THE
FOUR-MASTED BARQUE

The steel four-masted barque "Beatrice" (photo courtesy David R. MacGregor).

THE
FOUR-MASTED BARQUE

By

EDWARD BOWNESS *A.I.N.A.*

Model and Allied Publications,
Argus Books Ltd.,
Kings Langley, Herts

Made and printed in Great Britain by Butler & Tanner Ltd.,
Frome and London

CONTENTS

NOTE TO THIS EDITION

WHILE this book was originally written with the scale modeller in mind, it is also a fully detailed treatise on the four-masted barque in general, and as such will be of interest to all ship-lovers. Since the book was first written, some barque models in kit form, both wood and plastic, have become available, and most of the modelling techniques described here can be used to detail and improve kit-built models, though the full instructions given were originally intended for the scratch-builder.

PREFACE

THE square rigged sailing ship is generally considered to be one of the most beautiful things created by man. The graceful flowing curves of a ship's hull compel one to admire the artistry of the men who worked out the design and even more so to marvel at the skill of the men who framed the hull from such uncompromising material as steel plates and angle bars. In the dock the delicate tracery of the rigging, when seen against the sky, has a beauty which is now no more since the steamer has replaced it. At sea the tier upon tier of swelling canvas straining at the rigging and spars, and the whole ensemble swinging along in perfect harmony with the wind and the waves, in contrast to the steamship, which crashes her way through the seas, is the perfect embodiment of power and beauty in movement.

Curiously enough, in spite of the fantastic speeds which power-driven mechanisms have achieved, the sailing ship still stands as one of the most thrilling examples of speed. Probably the reason is that, as in the case of the racing yacht, the sailing ship attained the highest speeds which it was possible to obtain from the winds and that they were attained only when the gales were at their fiercest and only then by man taking risks and pitting his skill against the almost overwhelming forces of nature.

Whatever the reason, the sailing ship has still a great attraction for most of us, and as it is now next to impossible to see one on the sea or in port, the next best thing is to make a model. The four-masted barque has been chosen because, in the opinion of the author, this type represented the apex in the evolution of the sailing ship. For years it held its own against the steamship, and was only displaced when the marine engine reached a really high state of efficiency. The object of this book, in addition to describing the variations in the four-masted barque as a type, is to provide such information as will enable the would-be constructor to make a model which will be a correct copy of a four-masted barque, and which will recapture at least some of the grace and beauty of the original.

" Archibald Russell " setting sail

CHAPTER I

THE DEVELOPMENT OF THE TYPE

THE development of the sailing ship, which was spread over a period of about 5,000 years, culminated in the four-masted barque in the years between 1880 and 1910. At the beginning, and for centuries, development was extremely slow, and the three-masted ship was not introduced until the 15th century. Even then progress was still slow, but naval requirements accelerated their development and the great three deckers of the early 1800's were among the largest three-masted vessels ever built, especially as regards tonnage. However, considered purely as sailing ships they were inferior to the big three-masters built for passengers and trade to the colonies in the second half of the 19th century. The limit for this type was reached in the *Ditton* of 2,901 tons nett. She was built by T. R. Oswald & Co. Ltd., of Milford Haven, in 1891, and her dimensions were 311 ft. long × 42.3 ft. beam × 25.7 ft. depth. The *Ditton* and her sister ship, the *Speke*, were not a success as their gear was too big and heavy for a three-masted sailing ship. They would have been better if they had had four masts.

Even before the building of the *Ditton* the full rigged ship had developed in tonnage and dimensions to such an extent that designers considered the introduction of a fourth mast. Opinions were divided as to whether the fourth mast should be square rigged or not. In the early 1880's, a number of four-masted vessels were built, some barque rigged, i.e., with only fore-and-aft sails on the fourth or jigger mast, and others ship-rigged with yards on all masts. In service it was found that the barque rig was practically as efficient as the ship rig and it had the advantage of requiring a smaller crew. Later quite a number of four-masted ships were converted into four-masted barques and in many cases carried their ship-type jigger mast—which was built in three sections—long after the conversion had been made, as may be seen in many photographs taken at this period.

The first, and I believe the smallest, iron four-masted barque ever built was the *Tweedsdale*, built in 1877 by Barclay Curle, of Glasgow, to dimensions 244.4 ft. × 37.4 ft. × 22.6 ft., with a net tonnage of 1,403.

This was a smaller vessel than many three-masted ships of that time, but it was apparently a success as the type rapidly became popular. The largest four-masted barques ever built were the *Brilliant* and the *Daylight*, built by Russell & Company, Port Glasgow, in 1901 and 1902 for the Anglo American Oil Company, to carry case oil from America, see Fig. 5. The *Daylight* had a tonnage of 3,698 tons gross and 3,562 nett, and her dimensions were:—Length, 351.5 ft., beam 49.1 ft., and depth 28.2 ft. Between these extremes thousands of four-masted barques were built, ranging from 2,000 to 3,000 tons and in length from 270 to 320 ft. between perpendiculars. A number of very large ships were also built, and rigged as five-masted barques, but they seemed to be too big for a sailing ship and most of them came to an untimely end.

Apart from the question of size, a factor which helped to develop the sailing ship into an efficient carrier was the competition of the steamship. When the four-masted barque was first introduced the steamship was in its early stages and its engines were so uneconomical that it was impossible to carry sufficient coal for a long voyage and leave a margin for a paying cargo, and at the same time have engines large enough to meet all requirements. Most steamships carried sails, which were used when possible to eke out the coal. At this time the sailing ship maintained her supremacy, as she was on the whole faster, and was also cleaner and more economical than the steamship. However, the steam engine was being developed very rapidly for use both on land and sea, and before the end of the century, by means of higher boiler pressures and compound engines, the steamship gradually built up its supremacy over the sailing ship. For certain trades the sailing ship still possessed certain advantages, but the steamship, being comparatively independent of the vagaries of wind and weather, could be relied on to work to a time schedule, and thus her work could be planned with the minimum of loss through delays. Thus the sailing ship was superseded just when she had reached the point of her highest development. Therefore, for a ship modeller wishing to make a model of the sailing ship at the peak of her perfection, the choice must inevitably fall on the four-masted barque. It will, of course, be realised that the four-masted barque is merely a type of rig, and that within the limitations of that rig there is an almost endless number of variations to be considered. Also, during such a period of intensive development as that which produced and developed the four-masted barque there were a number of changes in the hull, especially as regards its convenience for handling and its comfort for the personnel who operated it.

Hull Details

Hull form was basically the same from about 1880, or a little earlier, to the end of the sailing ship era. The chief variations were to be found in the shape and style of the stem and its decoration, the flow of the lines under the counter, and the angle of the line between the knuckle and the upper edge of the counter. The amount of flare at the bows varied a little, and some ships had more curvature in the sheer line than others. These variations were, of course, the expression of the individualities of the different designers. If the lines of the actual ships to be modelled are unobtainable, all that the ship modeller can do is to adapt the lines of a typical ship to suit his requirements, allowance being made for any peculiarities the ship may be known to have possessed. Admittedly some ships were built on finer lines than others. The lover of a particular ship always considered that his favourite had finer lines than most. The usual tendency was for the builders to give their ships fuller lines as time went on, so as to provide greater carrying capacity as competition with steam became more serious. It is a fairly safe assumption that if one is modelling a four-masted barque of, say, 1880, without having access to its lines, it should be given finer lines than one of, say, 1895. A comparison between the lines of the *Archibald Russell* of 1905, see Figs. 14 to 17, and those of the *Lawhill* of 1890, Fig. 1, will illustrate the slight variations which existed between the lines of various four-masted barques during this period. Those of the *Lawhill* are a little fuller toward the ends of the vessel, but she is somewhat rounder at the bilges. The *Archibald Russell* has a sloping stem, whilst that of the *Lawhill* is almost vertical at the L.W.L., giving a slightly different form to the curve of the stem.

The counter of the *Archibald Russell* is longer than that of the *Lawhill* and consequently her buttock lines flatten out more than do those of the *Lawhill*. In comparing the lines of two vessels due regard must be paid to the position at which the sections are taken. For example, waterline 2 of the *Archibald Russell* should be compared with waterline 3 of the *Lawhill* and waterline 1 is comparable with a line midway between 1 and 2 of the *Lawhill*. There is no waterline on the *Archibald Russell* plan which compares with No. 4 on the *Lawhill*. The same applies to the buttock lines. There is no line on the *Archibald Russell* plan which compares with line *d* on the *Lawhill*. The waterlines and buttock lines may be safely ignored by the model maker. So long as the sections as shown in the body plan are correctly reproduced in the model, the other lines will automatically be correct. The waterlines and buttock lines are concerned only with the design and are a useful check on the correctness of the sections and give to the designer a clear indication of the particular

form of the hull. I remember one model which was completely spoiled
by its builder emphasising the hollows under the bow and counter in a
misguided attempt to embody the shape of the buttock lines. If he had
confined his attention to the sections in the body plan and ignored the
others, all would have been well.

With regard to dimensions, these are to be found in Lloyd's Register
or other similar list, due regard being paid as to whether the length given
is the overall length, the length between perpendiculars, or the length
on the load waterline. (L.W.L.) The system of measurement varied
between one registration authority and another, and on some points it
varied from time to time.

In addition to variations in the hull lines, there were other features
which must be noted by the model maker. Some of these are shown
in Fig. 2. Most four-masted barques had the floor of the poop and the
fo'c'sle on the same level as the main deck. This meant that in order
to give reasonable headroom the sides of the hull at these places had to
be raised above the level of the bulwark rail unless the bulwarks were
abnormally high. Harland & Wolff's ships—see " *A* " & " *B*," *Walter H.
Wilson* and *Sindia*—apparently had high bulwarks, as the line of the rail
is unbroken at the fo'c'sle while at the poop there is only a slight rise

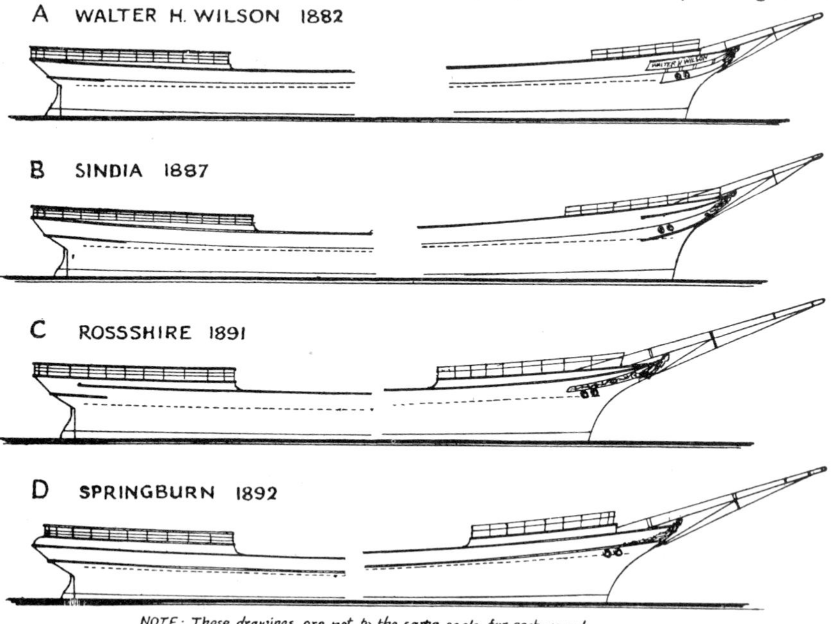

Fig. 2. Types of poop and fo'c'sle

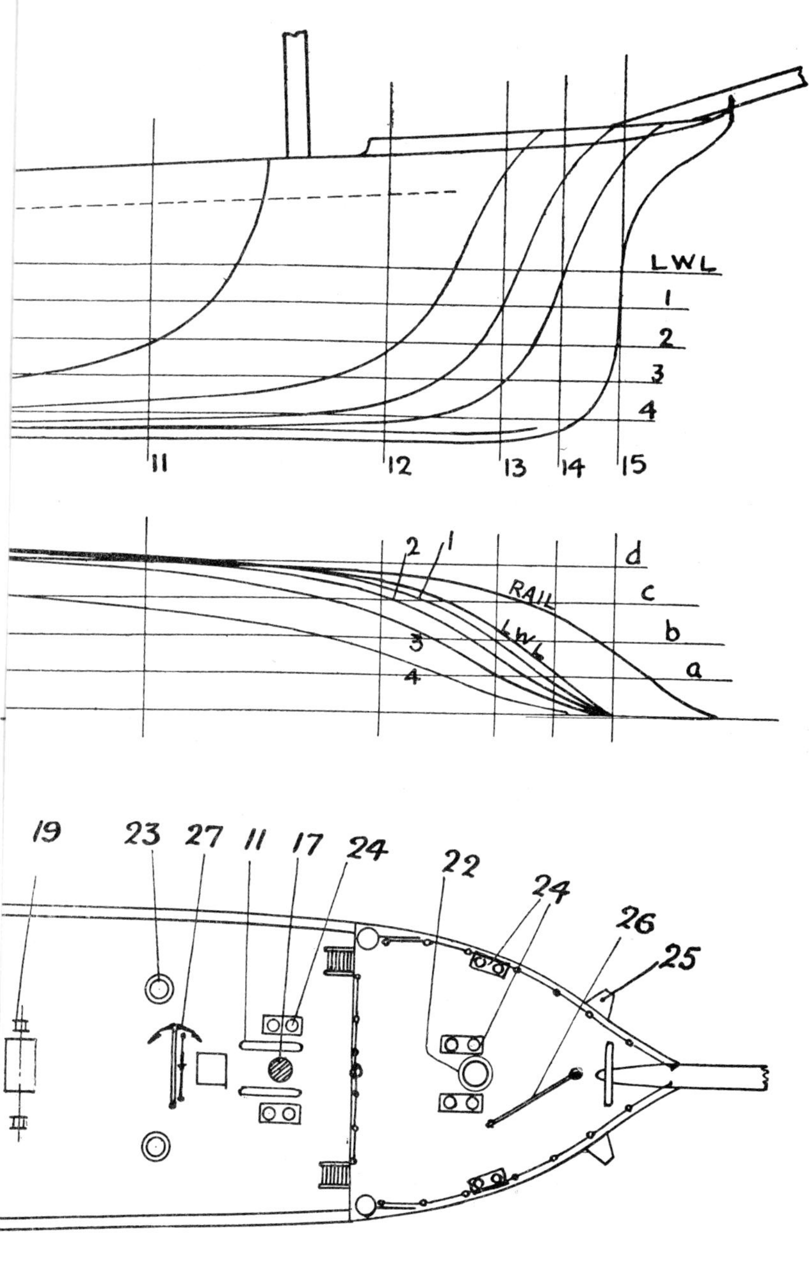

LWL
1
2
3
4
11
12
13
14
15
2
1
d
RAIL
c
LWL
b
3
4
a
19
23
27
11
17
24
22
24
26
25
200
EBowness '40

at the forward end, the poop deck being more nearly horizontal than the rail line. Actually the main deck and the floor of both the poop and the fo'c'sle follow a line which is more nearly level than the rail line, thus giving the necessary head room at these places. Barclay Curle, along with many other builders in the '80's and '90's, joined the bulwark rail to the poop deck by means of what was known as the " half-round." This actually was a quarter circle moulding from the upper edge of the bulwark strake to the edge of the poop deck which continued all round the poop, the poop rail lying well inboard from the ship's side. Good examples of this may be seen in the models of the four-masted barque *Pass of Melfort* and the ship *Blair Athole* in the Science Museum, South Kensington. At the fo'c'sle head the side plating was raised to give the necessary head room and formed what was termed the topgallant fore-castle, see *Springburn* " *D* " on Fig. 2. The poop in the *Rosshire*, " *C* " Fig. 2 is similar to that of the *Archibald Russell* and most of Scott's later ships. The t'gallant fo'c'sle is extended right forward to the figurehead, and the bowsprit is taken through the deck at an angle. In the *Sindia*, " *B*," the bowsprit is also taken through the fo'c'sle head at an angle whereas in the *Walter H. Wilson*, " *A*," the fo'c'sle head is terminated some distance aft of the figurehead, being stepped down about three feet to the upper rail of the decoration, the bowsprit passing through the narrow bulkhead thus formed. The front of the fo'c'sle head was sometimes carried straight across to the sides, but in other cases it was rounded off in plan, in the manner usually seen in the smart steam yachts of that time. See also *Mount Stewart*, Plate 31 and *Port Jackson*, Plate 35. In the *Archibald Russell*, Fig. 27 and the *Herzogin Cecilie*, Fig. 3, the fo'c'sle head was finished off straight across at its forward edge and the bowsprit taken through the step thus formed. This was a very popular arrangement and was to be found in a large proportion of the sailing ships of that time.

Deck Arrangement

The variations in the deck arrangement must be observed very carefully in building a model as it is these which, more than anything else will claim the attention of one who knows the ship, and especially of one who has sailed in her. Apart from the flying bridges which were not fitted in the early four mast barques, the deck arrangement of the *Archibald Russell*, see Fig. 27, is typical of that of most of the ships built from about 1880 to 1900, although it was by no means universal. In many ships the fo'c'sle was still used to house the crew, and in these cases there would only be one deck house forward of the mizzen mast. This deck house usually accommodated the boatswain, the carpenter, the sailmaker, the galley and the donkey boiler. Many ships had no house over the wheel, and in others again there was also no chart house on the poop. If the drawings of the ship to be modelled are available, these points will be apparent from the deck plan, but if not they can often be discerned from a photograph.

From about 1884, four-mast barques were occasionally built with a bridge deck. In this arrangement the midship's deck house was widened to extend to the sides of the ship, and its length increased to from 40 to 70 ft., making it large enough to house the entire personnel of the ship. This arrangement gave additional depth to the hull amidships which was its weakest point, and was found to add greatly to its strength. Before very long the authorities were so impressed with the value of this arrangement that it was made compulsory to provide such a bridge deck when the ratio of the length to the depth of the hull was $13\frac{1}{2}$ to 1 or more. This deck divided the main deck into two comparatively short wells, and thus when water was coming aboard in heavy weather the danger from flooded decks was greatly reduced.

This is clearly shown by a comparison of the decks in Plates 1 and 2. Plate 1 shows the long open deck of the *Olivebank* and one can realise the tremendous amount of water it could hold under certain conditions. Plate 2 shows the forward well deck of the *Pamir*. Admittedly the after well deck was somewhat longer than this, but even so, the advantage of the arrangement from this point of view is obvious. The bridge deck is easily seen in a photograph and must, of course, be followed in

Plate 1.   Main deck of " Olivebank " looking forward

Photo by G. Miller

Plate 2.   View from fo'c'sle head of " Pamir " showing bridge deck

Photo by J. Randall

Plate 3. " Wanderer " at Bristol

Plate 4. " Lyderhorn " in San Francisco Bay

modelling the ship. Plates 3, *Wanderer* ; 4, *Lyderhorn* ; 5, *Lawhill*, and 6, *Priwall* show good examples of this arrangement.

The *Wanderer* and the *Lyderhorn*, both Liverpool ships, had only a small whaleback at the stern, whereas the *Lawhill* and the *Priwall* had a normal poop with charthouse and wheelhouse on the deck and some accommodation under. This was the more usual arrangement in later years.

Plate 5. " Lawhill "

In the early years of this century, a number of ships were built in which the bridge deck was combined with the poop. These were all built either in Germany or Denmark, and were used as training ships. The best known ships of this type were the *Herzogin Cecilie*, plate 7, *Herzogin Sophie Charlotte*, *Viking* and *L'Avenir*, plate 8, all of which were four-mast barques. From the sailor's point of view this was the driest and most comfortable to work of all the types of sailing ships. All the braces and most of the running gear were led to this deck, and thus the bugbear of working the ship with flooded decks was a thing of the past. With the extra freeboard on the raised deck, bulwarks were unnecessary, except, perhaps, for a few feet at its forward end as in the *L'Avenir* and *Herzogin Cecilie* and open rails were provided. These allowed any seas that should chance to come aboard to run off freely, and the deck was

[*Photo by Marples*

Plate 6. " Priwall " in English Channel

Plate 7. " Herzogin Cecilie "

Photo by Grahame Farr

Plate 8. " L'Avenir " at Avonmouth in 1933

kept comparatively dry. The fittings on the raised deck varied in different examples of this type, but they can easily be made out from a photograph as they are not concealed behind the bulwarks. Plate 7, showing the *Herzogin Cecilie* and the photograph of the *L'Avenir*, Plate 8, show something of the deck arrangement of two different ships of this type.

The drawing, Fig. 4, affords an interesting comparison between the three principal types of hull. The *Port Jackson* shows the typical Clyde four-poster with long open decks. The half round between the upper edge of the bulwark strake and the edge of the poop deck will be noticed. The main deck house is situated aft of the foremast; in many ships it was situated aft of the main mast. The half deck is situated forward of the mizzen mast whereas later it was more usual to place it aft of this mast. An unusual feature of this ship was that she had outside channels for the shrouds which were set up with deadeyes and lanyards, probably the

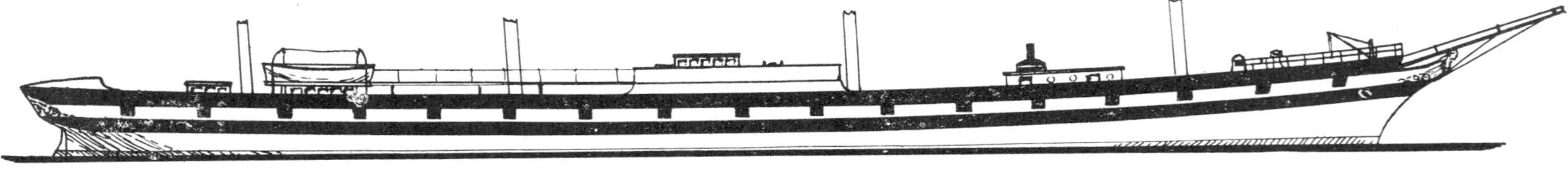

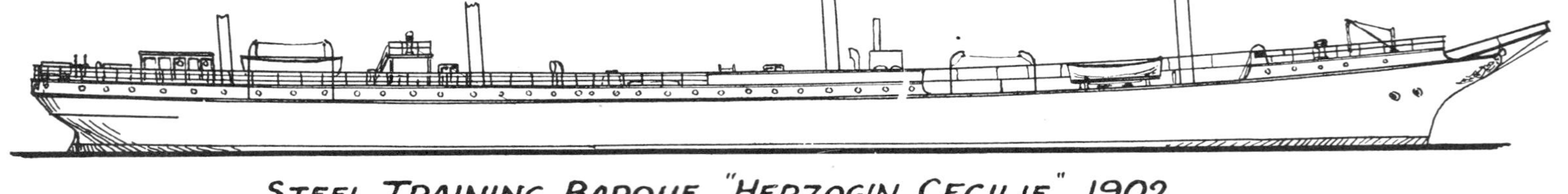

Fig. 4. Showing three principal types of hull

only four-masted barque with this arrangement. The anchorage for the shrouds was usually inboard at this time and bottle screws were used.

The *Wanderer* illustrates an early bridge deck ship. In this case the bridge deck was rather short and an additional deck house was provided between the main and fore masts. This housed only the galley and the donkey boiler; the captain, officers, apprentices and crew were accommodated under the bridge deck. A chartroom and wheel house was situated on this deck. An emergency steering gear and wheel was provided under the whaleback. The unusual arrangement of the plating at the stem head will be noted. In later vessels of this type the bridge deck was much longer, as was also the poop. Although the *Pamir* had the accommodation for the captain under the bridge deck, the poop had cabins for the first and second mates and the emergency steering wheel was placed amidships between them; the *Pamir* had no house in either of the well decks. At this time practically all the ships with bridge decks had a chart house and the main steering wheel on this deck. Later, however, the chart house was in many cases to be found in its old position on the poop, as shown in the *Forteviot* (later the *Bellands*) Plate 9, and the *Lawhill*, Plate 5 and Fig. 1.

Plate 9. " Forteviot " looking forward from poop

The *Herzogin Cecilie* shows the bridge deck combined with the poop. One can appreciate the greater freeboard and consequently the greater comfort of this type of ship. The chart house is situated in the usual place aft and the after wheel has no protecting house. The midship wheel by which the vessel is usually steered is placed aft of the main mast ; both wheels are double. The control platform with its standard compass is situated aft of the mizzen mast. The captain's cabin and officers' accommodation are right aft and the crew's quarters are amidships on the starboard side with the apprentices on the port and the galley and donkey boiler between them. In the *L'Avenir* the charthouse and wheel are arranged similarly to those of the *Herzogin Cecilie*. The midships wheel is just aft of the main mast, and the control platform with standard compass just aft of that.

The Americans built very few four-mast barques, although at about the turn of the century they purchased and operated a number of British-built vessels. Their name for the rig was " shipentine." After building the huge full rigger *Rappahannock*, of 3,054 tons, in 1889, the firm of A. Sewell & Co., of Bath, Maine, built three great " shipentines," the *Shenandoah*, 3,154 tons ; the *Susquehanna*, 2,591 tons, and the *Roanoke*, 3,347 tons. These were built of wood, as were practically all the American ships up to that time. The *Roanoke* was the largest wooden ship ever built in an American yard, with the sole exception of the *Great Republic*, of 1853. The wooden construction of American ships produced certain features not usually found on British ships. The stern had a flat or arched transom and the counter was much shorter than that in British ships. The stem was quite plain, being merely arched forward under the bowsprit. The rather exuberant figurehead of the earlier American ships had disappeared completely. Wooden handrails were fitted around the poop. The cabin floor was on a level with the main deck and the sides were set inboard from the bulwarks with a raised walk on each side similar to the arrangement found on the *Cutty Sark*. The wheel was enclosed in a large wheelhouse divided into two compartments which provided accommodation for the wheel, compasses and bell in the forward portion, and the rudder head, tiller and ropes, signal flags, buoys, etc., in the after portion. The photographs of *Shenandoah* and *Susquehanna* on Plates 10 and 11 show typical American " shipentines."

Rigging Details

I imagine every four-masted barque had double topsails, as these were introduced in 1865 and had become universal some considerable time before the introduction of four masts. Of the two most popular

Plate 10.   U.S. Shipentine " Shenandoah "

Plate 11.   U.S. Shipentine " Susquehanna "

Plate 12.   " Jordanhill "

rigs for the four-masted barque one was what was sometimes called the English rig, viz., single t'gan'sls and royals with a standing gaff on the jigger mast. See the frontispiece, and Plate 12, *Jordanhill*. The other, the so-called Scottish rig, had double t'gan'sls and royals, no spanker gaff and a jib headed spanker. Long doublings on the masts were also favoured by Scottish builders. The jib-headed spanker was usually set

Plate 13. " John Ena "

Plate 14. " Beatrice " ex " Routenburn "

from the lower mast top but sometimes it was set from near the mast head as shown in the photograph of the *John Ena*, see Plate 13. The early four-mast barques often set skysails above their royals as shown in the drawing of the *Routenburn* (See Fig. 5). In later years, after she was sold foreign and her name changed to *Beatrice*, the *Routenburn* was cut down as shown in Fig. 5 and Plate 14, the skysails and royals being dispensed with. It is said that this made scarcely any difference to her speed or sailing qualities. This rig, with nothing above the double t'gallants, was fitted to a number of ships in 1887 and onwards, and thus became known as the " Jubilee " rig. It was also known as the " stump t'gallant " rig, and ships thus fitted were termed " bald-headed." See also the photograph of the *Lawhill*, Plate 5, and the *Inverness-shire*, Plate 15. This rig was not very popular among those of the sailors and apprentices who prided themselves on their tall ships, but it was efficient and could be handled by a somewhat smaller crew, and thus was widely adopted. Curiously enough, toward the end of the sailing ship era there was a return to the use of royals.

The drawings in Fig. 5, being made to the same scale, give one a good idea of the development of the four-masted barque between the years 1881 and 1902. The *Daylight* was over 60 ft. longer than the *Routenburn* and her tonnage was nearly twice as great. Her masts were

Plate 15. " Inverness-shire "

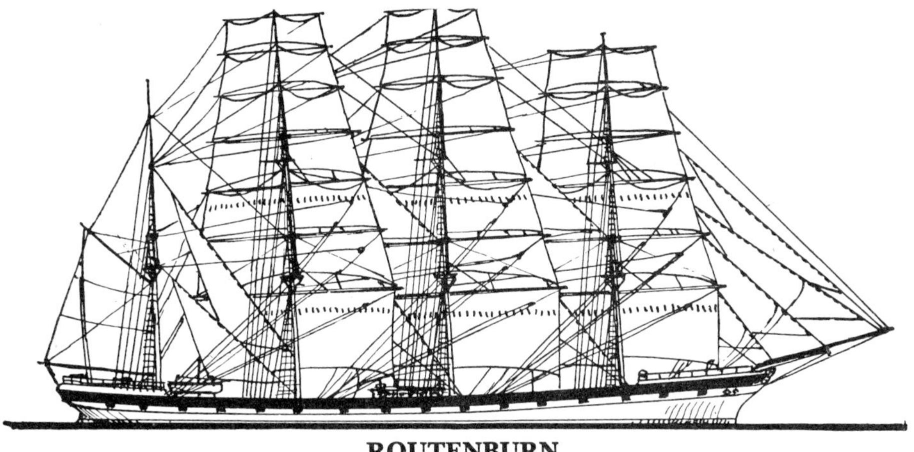

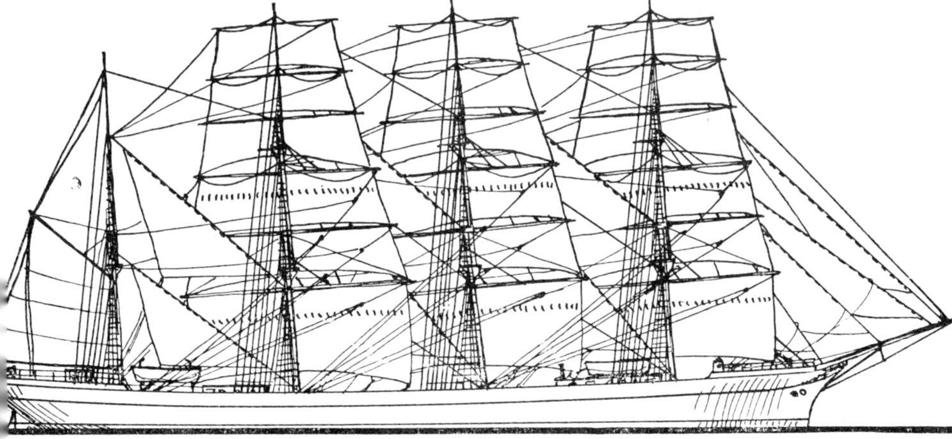

Fig. 5. Routenburn, Beatrice, Daylight drawn to same scale for comparison

practically the same height as the skysail masts of the *Beatrice*, her main
mast being 173 ft. deck to truck, with lower mast 75 ft. topmast 61 ft.
and t'gallant and royal masts 64 ft. with doublings 16 ft. and 12 ft.
respectively. The lower yards were 100 ft. long between plugs, topsail
yards 89 ft. and 81 ft., topgallant yards 74 and 63 ft., and royal yards
52 ft. long. The jiggermast was 153 ft. deck to truck and the spanker
boom 56 ft. long. The spike bowsprit was 61 ft. long.

A number of British four-mast barques were rigged with three skysails
above single topgallants and many of these, notably the *Owenee* and
Muskoka (both of 1891), *Queen Margaret* (1893) and the *Lynton* (1894)
were famed for both beauty and speed. Plate 16 shows the *Lynton*
being towed out to sea. The Liverpool barque *Wanderer*, made famous
by Masefield's book, had skysails on both fore and main, Fig. 8, and
single t'gallants when she first sailed, see Fig. 6, her fore and main masts
measuring 178 ft. 6 in. from deck to truck. Plate 3 gives one a good
impression of the height of her towering masts. The two four-mast
barques *Pegasus* and *Reliance* carried three skysails above double t'gallants
and thus had seven yards on their fore, main and mizzen masts.

In their four-mast barques the Americans invariably set skysails
over single t'gallants. Perhaps the finest example of the type was the
Shenandoah, built in 1890 (see Plate 10). She had a registered tonnage
of 3,154 on dimensions 299.7 ft. long, 39.1 ft. beam and 19.9 ft. depth.

Plate 16. "Lynton" leaving Liverpool

Fig. 6. " Wanderer " sail plan showing skysails on fore and main

Her mainyard was 94 ft. long and the trucks of her fore, main and mizzen masts are said to have towered 217 ft. above the deck. This seems somewhat excessive. Perhaps the height was taken from the mast step and not from the deck. Her spike bowsprit was of steel but all her other spars were of Oregon pine. In making a model of an American ship with wooden spars, the woolding or iron clamps for binding together the built lower masts must not be overlooked.

Masts and Spars

In the four-masted barque the lower masts were made of iron or steel, and in the earlier period, the topmasts were of wood. The mast was built in three sections, viz., lower mast, topmast and t'gallant mast which was in one piece with the royal mast and skysail mast (if any). The jigger mast was in two sections, as was usual with the three-masted barque. When steel began to be used for the topmasts and for spars generally, it was realised that the limitations due to the size of the average tree no longer existed, and that a steel spar could be made any desired length. Thus the lower and topmast could be made in one piece and the doubling could be dispensed with, resulting in a considerable saving of weight aloft. The photograph of the *Lawhill*, Plate 5, and of the *L'Avenir* Plate 8, show this arrangement. Many of the later German and French four-mast barques were fitted with masts of this type. The scheme, however, was by no means adopted universally, many vessels continuing to be built with their masts in three pieces. The jigger mast in the later four-mast barques was frequently made in one piece from the step to the truck. Examples from our illustrations are Plate 3, *Wanderer*, Plate 4 *Lyderhorn*, Plate 5 *Lawhill*, Plate 8 *L'Avenir*, Plate 13 *John Ena*, Plate 15 *Inverness-shire* and Plate 17 *Fascadale*. When the jigger mast was in two pieces crosstrees were fitted at the hounds, similar to those at the doubling of the topmast and topgallant mast. Although the doublings were dispensed with in some cases, the usual tops were retained on the square rigged masts, and the crosstrees on the jigger mast. These were, of course, necessary for spreading the rigging and handling the gear. A usual feature of the *Lawhill* was that her topgallant masts were fidded abaft the topmasts, see Plate 5. This scheme had certain advantages both in handling the sails and the gear, but it never became popular. Indeed, I cannot recall any other vessel whose masts were so arranged.

As the tonnage of the sailing ship was increased and larger hulls were built, the space from the stem head to the foremast was increased and the long overhanging jibboom was not so essential. It required but little change to extend the bowsprit as one spar to the required length, especially as, by this time, it was always made of steel. This spar became known as a spike bowsprit. Two notable four-mast barques, the *Port Jackson*, Fig. 4, and the *Beatrice*, Plate 14, had bowsprits with separate jibbooms, but these were exceptions and by far the greater number of four-mast barques had spike bowsprits.

The positions of the yards for the various rigs is a matter of considerable importance in a model. The point to be remembered is that some yards are fixed as to their height and the others must be hoisted when their sails are set. Referring to Fig. 7, the fixed yards are the lower yards, *A*, the lower tops'l yards *B*, and the lower t'gans'l yards *D*. All the others are hoisting yards. The lower yards are held by a crane or truss at the futtock band under the lower mast tops, the lower topsail yard is supported on the forward side of the lower mast cap by means of a truss or crane, and the lower topgallant yard is supported at the topmast cap by a similar fitting. These cranes were arranged so that the yard could swivel in both a horizontal plane for setting the sail to the wind, and a vertical plane for tilting the yard if necessary to clear a warehouse or other obstruction when the vessel was alongside a quay. When so tilted the yards are said to be " cockbilled." The hoisting yards are the upper topsail yard *C*, the upper topgallant yard *E*, the royal yard *F* and the skysail yard *G*. These are secured to the mast by a parrel which is a metal ring lined with metal, leather, or with hardwood to suit the material of which the mast on which it slides is made. At its forward side is a swivel giving movement in two directions in the case of

Plate 17. " Fascadale " under all plain sail

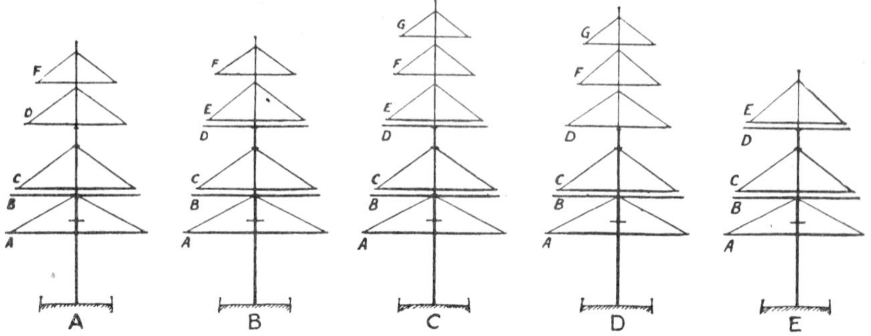

Fig. 7. Showing position of yards with sails furled

the upper topsail yard *C*. The remaining yards can turn in a horizontal direction only. In the later four-mast barques the parrel for the upper yards *E, F* & *G,* was replaced by a steel block which was made to slide in a metal track on the mast. When the hoisting yards are lowered their weight is taken by the lifts which, in the case of the upper yards which cannot be " cockbilled," are permanently shackled to eyes on the yards at the yardarms. When the sails are set and the yards hoisted these lifts hang in bights aft of the yard. A careful study of Figs. 77, 78 and 82 will make these various points quite clear.

The diagram, Fig. 7, shows the position of the yards when the sails are furled or stowed away. These positions, by the way, indicate very definitely the rig of the vessel, and also, in case of doubt, are a great help in identifying her. " *A* " shows the yards for a vessel with double tops'ls and royals over single t'gallants. " B," is for a vessel with double t'gallants and royals, " *C* " for the same rig with skysails. " *D* " shows skysails over single topgallants and " *E* " the stump t'gallant or jubilee rig. At one time, more particularly, in the days of the clippers, many shipmasters and mates prided themselves on having the yards equally spaced as nearly as possible. However, this fashion soon passed, and the more reasonable plan of letting the yards hang in their lifts, which after all were provided for this purpose, became general. This relieved the halliards and tyes of the weight of the yards and, by bringing down each yard to its lowest position, reduced the tendency for the ship to capsize when in harbour with the hold part or wholly empty.

The writer has seen a number of very fine ship models without sails in which the yards were hoisted to the positions they would occupy if the sails were set. This is a mistake, however attractive it may look to some people, as this condition never happened in a real ship.

Before leaving the subject of the yards it should be mentioned that

many ship modellers overlook the difference in the arrangement of the
buntlines and clewlines between those of the earlier four-mast barques
and those of the later ones.   I had sent to me once a set of photographs
of a very fine model of the clipper *Caliph,* which was built by an American
Naval officer, and in which, although everything else was practically
perfect, the rigging was arranged for clewing the square sails to the yard
arms instead of to the quarters, a system which was quite unknown until
many years after the *Caliph* was lost.   Such a mistake is so prominent
that it spoiled completely the appearance of the model.   Fig. 8 illustrates
the earlier arrangement.   In this the leading blocks for the clew lines
are located on the yard at the quarters, which are about two-thirds in
from the yard arms, and when the sail is furled, the clews or lower corners
of the sail are hauled up to these blocks.   To allow of this, the sheets,
which are also attached to the clews of the sail, are paid out and remain
visible when the sail is furled.   If the sail is taken off altogether, as it
would be for a prolonged stay in port, the clew lines are hauled up to
their respective blocks and the sheets shackled on to them just outside
the blocks.   The outer buntline was attached to the leech or outer edge
of the sail as may be seen in the photograph of the *Fascadale,* Plate 17,
when it becomes known as a leechline.   When it is hauled in, on furling
the sail, the sail is stowed as shown in Fig. 8, the greater bulk of the
sail being at the centre of the yard with the remainder tapering toward

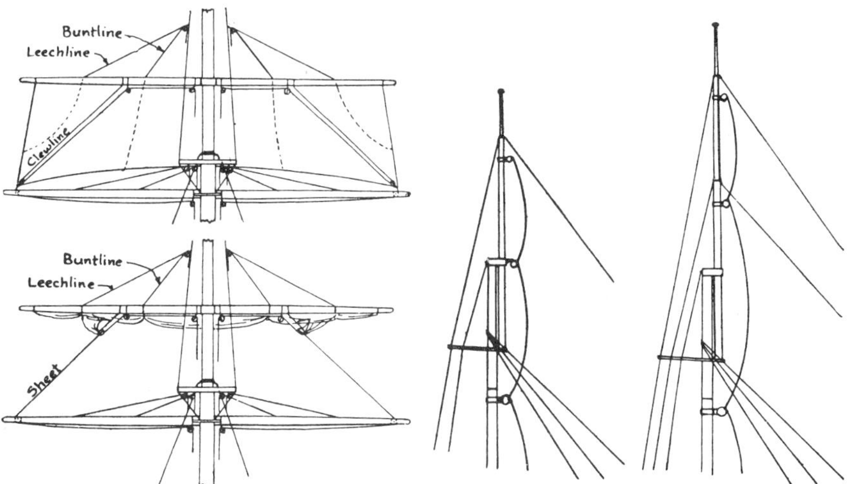

Fig. 8.   Leech lines and clewlines with
sail furled to bunt

Fig. 9.   Left: Double t'gans'ls   Right:
Royal over single t'gans'l'

each yard arm. This was considered the sign of a smart ship at one time—as it emphasised the tapering of the yards.

In the later arrangement the leechlines were done away with, the leading blocks for the clew lines were located at the yard arms, and the buntlines hung more or less vertically from their blocks as shown in Plate 6 (*Priwall*). When the sail was furled it was drawn up vertically for the full width of the sail and stowed alongside the jackstay—a rail fitted along the upper surface of the yard. Owing to the sail being wider on its foot than at its head the clews projected a little and were allowed to hang down at each end, being attached to the clewline and the sheet at the point where they meet, and which is marked *X* on Fig. 82. A study of Fig. 82 should make this clear. The photographs, Plate 3 (*Wanderer*), Plate 5 (*Lawhill*), Plate 15 (*Inverness-shire*), and several others show sails furled in this way.

The upper topsail yard is fitted with downhauls which are rove through blocks at the yardarms (see 72 in Fig. 82) to assist in lowering the yard when reefing or furling the upper topsail. When double t'gan'sls were introduced, similar downhauls were provided to assist in lowering the upper t'gan'sl yard. When the sails were clewed up to the quarters these downhauls were the only lines running down from yard-arm to yard-arm. Later, when the sails were clewed up to the yard-arms, we had lines running down from yard-arm to yard-arm from the uppermost yards to the lower yards. During the transition stage the royals and skysails were often clewed up to the quarters while the lower sails were clewed up to the yardarms. In the frontispiece, which is a photograph of the *Carradale*, built in 1889, the royals are shown with leech lines for clewing up to the quarters while the remaining sails have buntlines for clewing up the sails to the yardarms. When a model is shown without sails these points become very noticeable, and should, therefore, be given the greatest consideration.

Reef points were in common use on square sails up to the early years of this century, at which time they were usually fitted on the courses and the upper topsails. With divided topsails and t'gallants and the reduced crews of this period, the tendency to furl sails rather than reef them grew, until reef points were finally discarded. None of the big German four-mast barques had them, and they were gradually discarded in British ships.

It will be realised that the fore-and-aft stays must be attached to the masts so as not to interfere with the hoisting of the yards. The lower and topmast stays are fitted around the mast at the doublings. The upper stays require a little thought. For example, with the stump t'gallant rig there is only one stay on the t'gallant mast whereas with a royal over a single t'gans'l there are two. (See Fig. 9.) Strictly speaking the second rig has a t'gallant mast and a royal mast (although they are invariably made as one spar), with a stay at the head of each, whereas the stump t'gallant rig has only a t'gallant mast and therefore one stay.

Where sails are divided, as in topsails and t'gan'sls, the foot of the upper sail is cut with little or no roach (or arch) as there are no stays to be avoided. The only purpose of the roach at the foot of a square sail is to clear the stays below it and the curve should be only just sufficient for this purpose. Sail area is not sacrificed without reason.

Of the fore and aft sails, the jibs and staysails call for no particular comment. The headsails consisted almost invariably of the fore-topmast staysail, the inner and outer jibs and the flying jib. The flying jib was hanked to the fore-topgallant stay. The remaining three sails were hanked to their respective stays which came down from the fore topmast head to the bowsprit (see Fig. 3). Several staysails were carried between the masts from the stays, taking their names from the stays to which they were hanked. Fig. 3 shows a typical layout, although in different ships there were different arrangements.

There were many variations of the spanker and jigger topsail. Fig. 10 shows a number of those which were to be met with. (A) shows the most common arrangement and one which was usual in both British and American ships. (B) Shows the sail where there is no spanker gaff. The small monkey gaff set higher up the mast was used for signalling purposes. The sail was sometimes set up to the jigger mast-top and sometimes to the cap. Sometimes, particularly in U.S. ships, a topsail was used with this sail, reaching from near the mast-head to the after end of the boom. In (C) the spanker is made as one huge sail reading from the boom to the masthead, as already mentioned in the case of

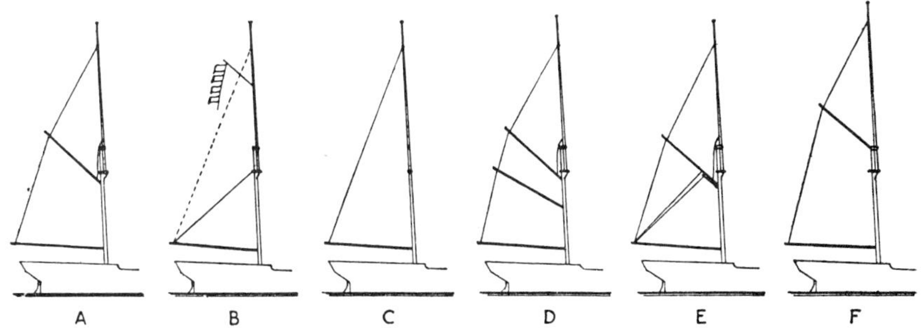

Fig. 10. Various types of spanker and jigger topsail

the *John Ena*, Plate 13.   The large German four-mast barques were frequently fitted with two spanker gaffs, an upper and a lower, as shown in (*D*).   They were rigged with topping lifts from the masthead to the gaffs, and on to the boom, and each gaff was provided with vangs. (*E*) shows the storm sail which was used in many four-mast barques. It was usually jibheaded, but was often provided with a short spar or jackyard at the head as shown in the drawing.   This sail was sometimes augmented by an additional sail which was triangular and which was carried out to the peak of the gaff, and sheeted home to the after end of the boom.   The big Liverpool four-mast barques often carried their standing gaffs at the lower mast cap, as shown at (*F*).   Where the jigger mast was a single pole, it was carried at the point where the cap would have been.   This made for a larger spanker and a smaller gaff topsail. The large spanker must have been a tremendous sail to handle, see *Wanderer*, Plate 3 and Fig. 6, and *Lyderhorn*, Plate 4.

CHAPTER II

PLANNING THE MODEL

HAVING studied the four-masted barque as a type, and having considered the variations which existed between different examples of that type, we are now in a position to appreciate the special points of the vessel in which we may be particularly interested, and which we would like to model. Obviously, it is out of the question in a book of this size, to describe how to make a model of every variation of the four-masted barque, so we have taken a typical example for the purpose of explaining in detail how to make a model, pointing out as we proceed, any special problems which may arise in modelling a vessel different from the one we have chosen as an example.

The example we have chosen is the *Archibald Russell*, see Fig. 18. There are several reasons for our choice. Personal knowledge is one ; I was able to pay several visits to this ship in the spring of 1930 and in 1931, when she was discharging in London. At that time she was in the Australian grain trade, in which she distinguished herself with several smart passages, and was under the command of Captain Lindfors. While on board I took a number of photographs around the decks, some of which are reproduced in the book. Later a series of blueprints from the builders came into my possession. From these I was able to obtain accurate dimensions and to clear up many doubtful points. Another reason for our choice is that she was the last big square rigger to be built on the Clyde, and therefore represents a mature example of her type, at any rate in its simpler form. She is just a plain straightforward Clyde four-poster with no refinements, no bridge deck, no mechanical power save for the usual donkey engine for the windlass, no brace or halliard winches, and no fancy gear about her rigging.

She is a typical example of the thousands which were built, and in addition is a noteworthy example of the beauty of the sailing ship.

This part of the book has been developed from a series of articles by the writer published in the " Ship-modeller's Corner " of *The Model Engineer* during 1945 and 1946. The articles were written to enable the model-maker, who may have no particular knowledge of sailing ships, to make a worth-while model. There is nothing more discouraging to a model maker than to find as his model progresses, during which time he

Plate 18. " Archibald Russell " at Seattle

has, of course, been consciously or unconsciously accumulating information, that some of the information on which he commenced his model is incorrect. It is then too late to make basic changes and the remainder of his work on the model is being put into something which is not quite accurate. It is the aim of this book to prevent this. The model-maker with no specialised knowledge of sailing ships may safely go ahead with a model to these particulars, assured that any information he may come across during the building of his model will only confirm the particulars here presented.

The Prototype

The *Archibald Russell* was a steel four-mast barque built by Scotts of Greenock, in 1905, for Messrs. Hardie & Co., of Glasgow. Her leading dimensions as given in Lloyd's Register were 291.3 ft. long, 42.9 ft. beam, 24 ft. depth. She had a poop 41 ft. long and a topgallant fo'c'sle 36 ft. long. Her gross tonnage was 2,354 and net tonnage, 2,048. Although not one of the largest of four-mast barques, she was always considered one of the most handsome. Compared with some of the larger barques, she had rather fine lines, but being built for cargo capacity rather than for speed, her lines are not so fine as those of the early clippers. With regard to sail plan, she always carried three royals over double topgallants, and was never reduced to the bald-headed rig, as was the case with so many of the later sailing ships. She was bought by Captain Erikson, of Mariehamn, in 1924, and in carrying grain from Australia during her later years, proved herself one of his fastest ships; she made the best passage for 1929.

In her early years she had the painted ports which were usual for most large ships in those days. (See Plate 18.) During her first years under the Erikson flag, she was painted white, and so long as the paint was kept in good order, she looked a queen amongst her sisters. About 1933, however, probably from considerations of economy, she was painted black, and continued in that colour until the outbreak of the war.

At that time she was in Hull unloading a grain cargo and was not allowed to put to sea. When Finland joined the Axis Powers she was taken over by the Navy, and for some years was used as a food depot by the Government. Late in 1946 she was towed to the Tyne and moored at Dunston where she was ultimately broken up.

What a pity that someone could not have been found to restore her to her former glory, as the late Captain Dowman did with the *Cutty Sark*, so that future generations would have had the opportunity of seeing what the big sailing ship looked like at the peak of her perfection.

Fig. 11. Hull and rigging model of " Archibald Russell "

The Model

But to get back to our model—the one I propose to describe will be painted in her original colours with black bulwark strake, a line of black ports on a white strake, a black line and light-grey to the water line. The under-water body will be painted red, the usual colour for the anti-fouling composition of that day. The model will have a complete hull and no sails, so that the delicate, intricate beauty of the rigging may show to full advantage. I have often argued that a model showing the under-water body should be shown without sails, whilst the water-line model looks better with sails. For the sake of those who prefer to build a water-line model, we include the necessary instructions. Generally speaking, with the exception of the sails, there is very little difference in the making of either type, and either would make an interesting and attractive model. To help the prospective builder to decide which of the two types he should make, I have prepared a sketch of each (See Figs. 11 and 12.) The model in full sail, heeling over to the breeze, and with the waves just lapping over the lee rail, certainly makes an attractive picture, but there is a very real fascination in the serene dignity and beauty of the other type.

Fig. 12. Waterline model of " Archibald Russell " in full sail

The scale of the model is important. Dockyard and shipbuilder's models are usually made to the scale of $\frac{1}{4}$ in. = 1 ft. This produces a model of a size more suitable for a museum than for the average private house. $\frac{1}{8}$ in. = 1 ft. is a very convenient scale, but a model to this scale is still rather large for the present-day small house, especially if one desires to possess more than one ship model. For our model we decided on the scale of $\frac{1}{16}$ in. = 1 ft. The actual size works out at 22 in. from the spanker boom to the tip of the bowsprit, $11\frac{3}{4}$ in. from keel to truck, the lengths of the lower yards being $5\frac{1}{2}$ in. At this scale it is possible to include a considerable amount of interesting detail and, if it is put in a glass case, as it should be to protect it from dust and damage, the case is still of a convenient size for the average house. The detail in the model, as described in the book, will produce a very realistic and very satisfying model, and the work is well within the capacity of the average ship modeller. If, however, the builder wishes to make a larger or a smaller model, the instructions and drawings will still be found to be very useful, and the builder can put in more or less detail as his skill and experience dictates. It may be mentioned that several larger models have been built from these instructions, one being three times the size, giving a hull length of $58\frac{3}{8}$ in. overall. The hull of this model was described and illustrated in *Model Ships and Power Boats* for November, 1951.

Plate 19. " Cutty Sark " model to scale 1/16 in. = 1 ft.

The methods recommended throughout this book are based on those I used in building a $\frac{1}{16}$ in. scale model of the *Cutty Sark* shortly before commencing work on the book. Also, the amount of detail suggested here is approximately the same as that which I included in the model. To give readers an idea of the effect produced by this amount of detail, a photograph of the model is reproduced as Plate 19.

Hull Lines and Dimensions

Before commencing work on the model of the *Archibald Russell* the builder would be well repaid by a careful study of the lines. (See Figs. 13 to 17.) The cross section is full, but not too box-like. The floor has a considerable amount of dead-rise and the sides have a reasonable tumble-

.home. Fore and aft the ship has a beautiful sheer line, which is further emphasised by the line of painted ports. The ends are full, as befits a carrier, but they are beautifully shaped. To enable the modeller to get them correct and so to preserve the beauty of the hull, the lines at both bow and stern are drawn the actual size of the model. (See Figs. 16 and 17.) Very few models of sailing ships preserve the exquisite beauty of the stern. The counter is either too long or too short, and the angle between the underside of the counter and the sternpost is incorrect. The underside of the counter should flow naturally from the lines of the plating. Then again, the angle at the knuckle of the counter must be copied very carefully. The same remarks apply more or less to the shape of the stem and the flare at the bows. In an iron or steel ship the beauty of the bows depends entirely on the form, and receives no assistance from head rails or decorated trail boards, as was the case with the wooden ships. Therefore, the greatest care must be taken to ensure that the model is made correctly to the lines, and that the curvature of the stem is copied faithfully.

The body plan, or midship section, Fig. 15, is drawn the full size of the model and the shape at each of the stations is given. If a series of templates is made from these lines and the hull carefully carved to them at their respective stations, and the intervening portions faired away to flow smoothly into these sections, the result will be a hull which reproduces all the grace and beauty of the original.

The sheer plan, or side elevation, Fig. 13, gives the location of the stations, Nos. 1 and 18 being the perpendiculars between which the length of the ship is measured. When the length is given as being " between perpendiculars " the after perpendicular is taken at the after side of the sternpost. The forward perpendicular is taken at the point where the line of the stem at the cut-water, if produced, would intersect the line of the main deck. The stations are spaced more closely towards each end, as there the shape changes more rapidly.

Adding the dimensions for the distance between the stations 1 to 18 we get 17 17/32 in. as the length between the perpendiculars. This, at our scale of $\frac{1}{16}$ in. = 1 ft., equals a length of 280 ft. 6 in. The overhang at the stern is 12 ft. and at the bow 19 ft., giving dimensions of $\frac{3}{4}$ in. and $1\frac{3}{16}$ in. respectively, and an overall length of 19 15/32 in., which equals 311 ft. 6 in. Where a ship has a figurehead it is usual to give the overall length from the stern to the end of the plating forward, and not to the tip of the figurehead. The *Archibald Russell*, however, has no figurehead, only a scroll, so we have taken the length over the scroll, as the plating was taken practically to the end of the scroll.

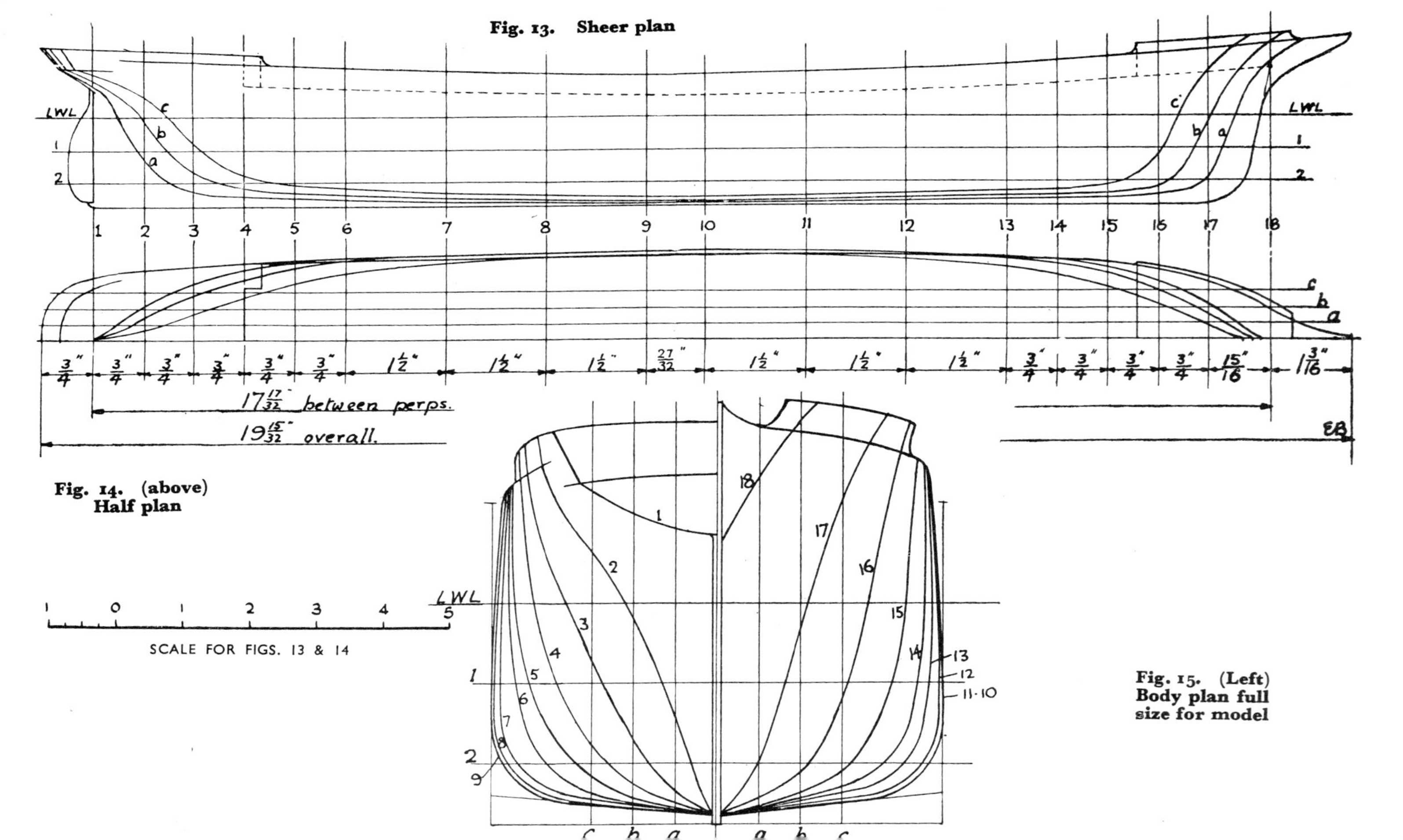

Fig. 13. Sheer plan
Fig. 14. (above) Half plan
Fig. 15. (Left) Body plan full size for model
SCALE FOR FIGS. 13 & 14
17 17/32" between perps.
19 65/32" overall.

It will be noticed that the length between perpendiculars does not agree with the length already given, and which was taken from Lloyd's Register. In Finnish and Italian ships the length is always taken as being the length overall, and, the *Archibald Russell* being a Finnish ship this difference may or may not have been taken into account when she changed hands and was re-registered. Again, she was originally classed in the British Corporation and not in Lloyd's, and the B.C. method of measurement may have been different from Lloyd's. I must confess I have been unable to reconcile these differences. However, the builder's drawings give a water-line length of 278 ft. and our drawings are prepared in accordance with this ; so I feel justified in assuming that our drawings are consistent with the ship as she was built.

The moulded breadth of the ship is 42.9 ft., so in our model it will be 2¹¹⁄₁₆ in. The depth is rather more involved. The moulded depth is measured from the top of the keel to the level of the upper deck beam at the gunwale. As these figures do not help much with the model, we have assumed a draught of 22 ft. (actually it was 21 ft. 7½ in.) and the height from the L.W.L. to the rail amidships as being 10 ft., giving dimensions for the model of 1⅜ in. and ⅝ in. respectively. The stemhead and the forward edge of the topgallant forecastle are approximately 20 ft. (1¼ in.) above the L.W.L. and the poop deck at the taffrail 18 ft. (1⅛ in.)

Definitions

A shipmodelling correspondent asked for a few explanations with regard to the hull lines of the *Archibald Russell*. He said : " I do not understand the curved lines *a*, *b*, and *c*." These are buttock lines, and line *c* represents what the edge of the surface would look like if the portion of the hull outside line *c* were cut away. Similarly line *b* represents the edge if the thickness *c* to *b* were next cut away, and line *a* the outline of the edge if the thickness *b* to *a* were removed. To the experienced eye these lines give a very good idea of the form of the hull.

He also wished to know the meaning of the expressions " Counter," " Dead-rise," and " Tumble-home."

The " Counter " is the portion of the hull which lies aft of the sternpost.

" Dead-rise " is the amount of upward slope in the floor of the vessel. It is represented in the Body Plan, Fig. 15, by the lines immediately above the lowest horizontal line, which slope upward and outward on each side. A steamer usually has no dead-rise, having a flat bottom, whereas a yacht or a clipper has a considerable amount.

" Tumble-home " is the inward slope of the sides of the ship, and is represented in the Body Plan before-mentioned, by the space between the vertical lines which are carried up to the rail level on each side, and the outline of the hull at stations 9, 10 and 11.

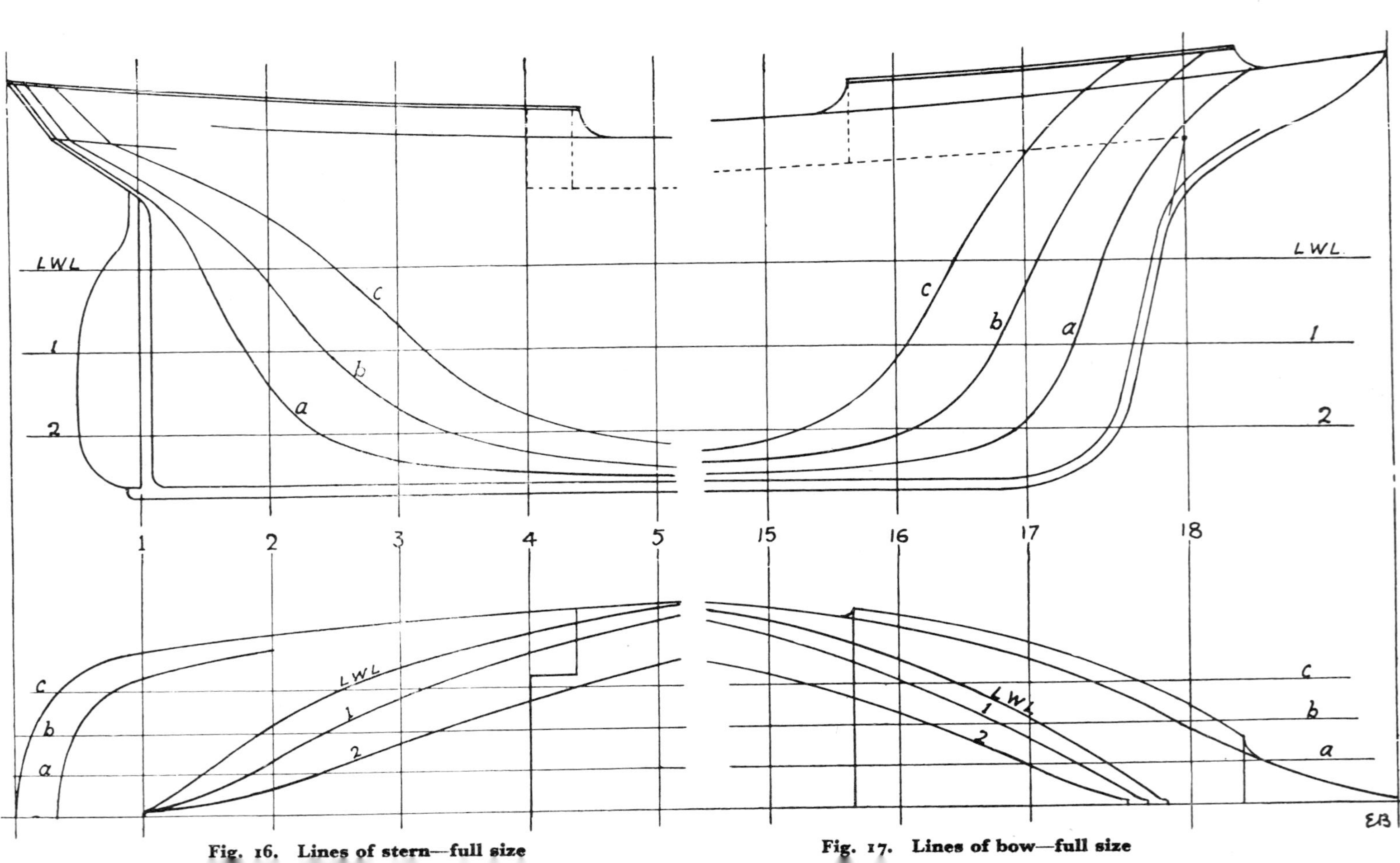

Fig. 16. Lines of stern—full size   Fig. 17. Lines of bow—full size

CHAPTER III

SHAPING THE HULL

THE size of material required will be 19¾ in. × 2⅞ in. × 2¾ in. Some will prefer to carve the entire hull out of one block, while others will prefer to make the poop and fo'c'sle separately. In this case the block required would measure 19¾ in. × 2⅞ in. × 2¼ in. The ideal material is, of course, yellow pine, but lime, red pine, American whitewood, or any reasonably soft wood with a close straight grain, would be suitable. Having procured a suitable block of wood, the first thing to do is to plane it true to the dimensions given.

Transferring the Lines

Next, draw on the two side faces the outline of the hull as given in the side elevation. The outline at the bow and stern can be traced direct from the full-sized details. The rudder may be formed out of the solid block or, if preferred, it may be made as a separate piece. At this scale it is probably better to form it out of the solid, especially in view of the extension of the keel which forms the pivot for its lower end.

Great care should be taken with the shape of the stem. In the early clippers this was based on the shape which had been handed down from the days of the wooden warships and consisted of two similar curves, reversed, as shown at *A* and *B* in Fig. 18. By the close of the era of the sailing ship, it had been modified in that the radius of the upper curve was reduced and that of the lower curve increased as shown at *C*, Fig. 18. This is one of the little things that mean so much to the one who really knows and loves ships.

With regard to the sheer line, note that its lowest point is a little aft of amidships, say midway between stations 8 and 9, and that the amount of rise is greater forward than aft. Try to get a nice smooth curve for the sheer line, taking the height at the ends from the full-sized drawing and making it, at its lowest point, exactly 2 in. above the bottom of the keel. Ignore the raised fo'c'sle and poop until you have drawn the sweep of the sheer line from station 2 to the tip of the scroll at the bow in one perfect curve. Then draw the poop parallel to the sheer line and a bare 3/16 in. above it. The fo'c'sle head is the same height at its after end,

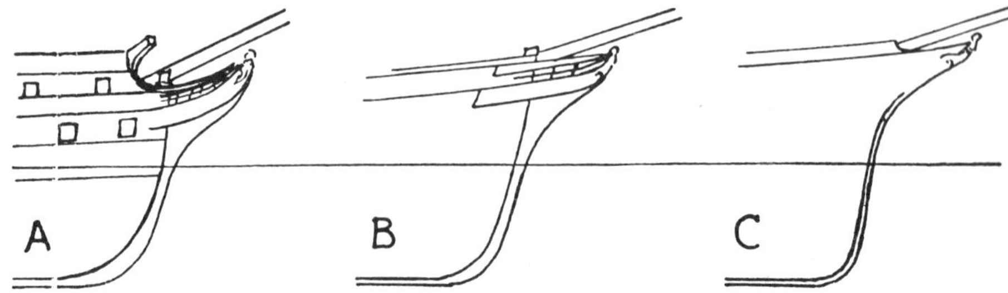

Fig. 18. Comparison of stem outlines

but about 1/32 in. less at its forward end. The outline of the hull could very well be drawn first on a strip of tracing paper, tracing the ends from the full-sized drawing and completing the sheer lines with splines and weights if you are the fortunate possessor of such things.

To transfer the lines to the block of wood, the best method is to lay the tracing paper drawing with the surface on which the pencil lines are drawn in contact with the wood, and go over them with a firm pencil. This leaves a faint pencil line on the wood. Then lay the paper on the other side of the block with the new pencil lines in contact with the wood, and go over the original drawing with a firm pencil. This also leaves a faint pencil line on the wood and, as in each case it is drawn from the same outline, the outlines on the wood will correspond exactly to each other. It cannot be otherwise, as, if the pencil wanders off the line, there will be no line underneath it at that point to be transferred to the wood. The method is easier to perform than to explain, but is well worth the trouble of learning.

Preliminary Shaping

Having marked the wood on both sides, the block should be cut across and squared until it assumes the shape shown in Fig. 20. A jig-saw or a band-saw can be very useful here. Failing a jig-saw, an ordinary tenon-saw will be very helpful, and in the outline between the poop and fo'c'sle, where there is a considerable amount to be removed, a series of sawcuts, as shown in Fig. 19, will be a help in removing the surplus material.

A centre-line should now be drawn on the ends and on the upper and lower surfaces of the block, and an outline showing the maximum width drawn on the upper and lower surfaces. It will be noted that the maximum width at the stern is at the line of the poop deck, amidships it is well below the L.W.L., and forward it is at the edge of the flare at the fo'c'sle head. These outlines should be transferred to the block by the method already described, first tracing the line on one side of the centre

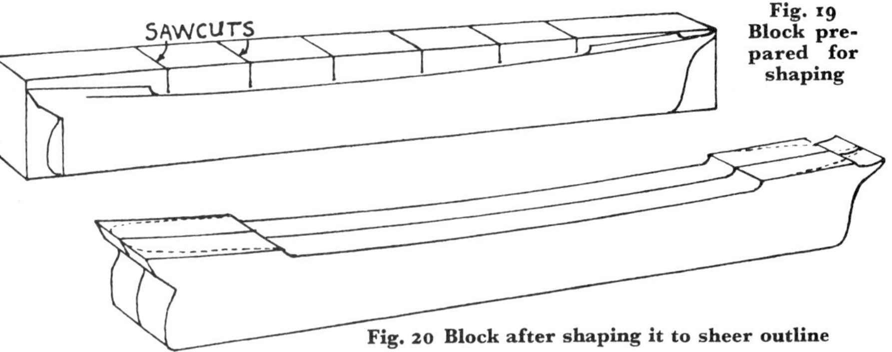

Fig. 19
Block pre-
pared for
shaping

Fig. 20 Block after shaping it to sheer outline

line and then turning over the paper to trace the outline on the other side of the centre line, thus ensuring perfect symmetry. A slight allowance must be made for the increased length due to the curvature of the surface of the deck.

When the block has been cut away to these outlines the stations 1 to 18 should be marked off carefully and a line drawn all round the block at each station. If the block is placed on a flat surface, the vertical lines can be drawn by means of a set-square, and then joined across the upper and lower surfaces. Number each station.

Final Shaping

Having completed the preliminary shaping of the block for the hull, the next operation is to carve the outside to the final shape, as indicated in the drawing of the lines, Figs. 13 to 17. First, we require a set of templates for checking the form at the stations which are numbered 1 to 18. Only sixteen templates are required, as the sections at stations 9, 10 and 11 are practically the same, and one template will be sufficient for these: there is a slight difference in the height, but if the template is made to suit No. 11, which is the highest, it can be used for the other two. The templates should be cut out of Bristol board or other good quality cardboard, or they might even be cut from 1-mm. or 1/32-in. plywood. Fig. 21 shows the general shape of the templates. From *A* to *B* the shape should be copied very accurately from the hull sections, as should also the distance from *A* to the centre line at *C*. When cutting, as the shape of the hull approximates the shape indicated on the appropriate template, the template must be applied more frequently so as to avoid cutting too deeply into the wood. With regard to the sections between stations 6 and 13, a good plan is to cut the sections to fit their respective templates as a series of gentle hollows, and then to fair them into one another by taking longitudinal cuts with a wide chisel, working from amidships towards each end, so as not to go against the grain of the wood.

Great care must be taken not to cut away the projecting keel, or to reduce the thickness of the stem or the deadwood at the stern more than is necessary. These should be thin, but must be of approximately equal thickness from the scroll at the stem right round to the point where the sternpost enters the hull under the counter. Some ship modellers prefer to make the keel as a separate strip and from somewhat harder wood. This method has certain advantages, but, personally, when making a small model, I find that, if the keel is made a little wider than scale size in the earlier stages, it is easy to finish it to the correct thickness in the

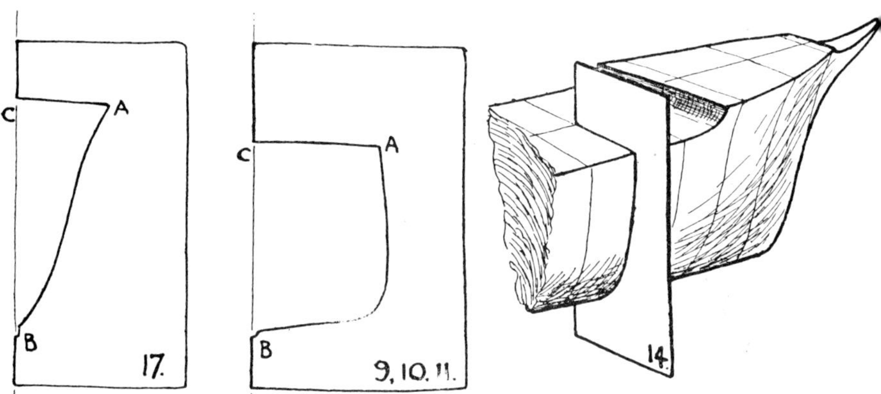

Fig. 21. Templates and their application

final stages ; and the difficulty of making a nice joint between the keel and the stem and the sternpost is avoided.

If the sheer line is cut correctly on the block before starting to shape the sides, the height of A above B measured vertically on the templates should give a perfectly straight line at the keel between stations 1 and 17. Similarly, if the block is made to the correct maximum width at each station, the edge of the templates will be found to line up exactly with the centre-line when the block is cut to fit the outline between points A and B.

Carving the Deck

We are now ready to cut out the well of the main deck. Its extent is indicated on the plan views in the hull lines (see Fig. 14), the break of the poop being between stations 4 and 5, and that of the fo'c'sle between stations 15 and 16. Its depth is indicated by dotted lines in the elevation or sheer draft, Fig. 13. Here again is a matter for personal preference as

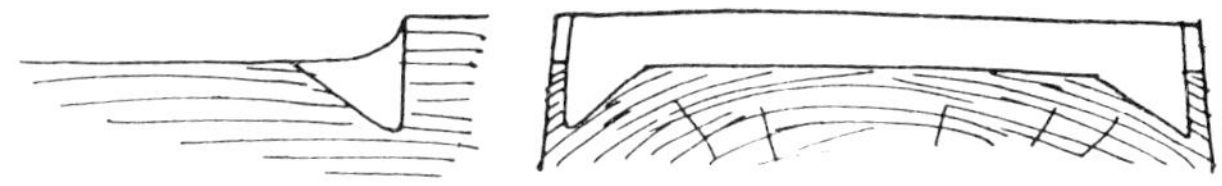

Fig. 22. Carving the deck

to whether the builder fits the bulwarks separately, or forms them from the solid by cutting away the wood between them down to the deck level. I consider the first method is more suitable for a model of a wooden ship, where the sheer line follows very closely the line of the deck ; but for a model of an iron or steel hull, where the sheer line is a foot or so above the level of the deck, see Fig. 27, it is perhaps better to carve the well of the deck from the solid. There will then be no joint to break the smoothness of the sheer strake. As this is painted white and forms the base for the line of ports, it is important that its surface is smooth and unbroken.

Cutting out the well from the solid calls for sharp tools and a steady hand and eye. First cut vertically downwards at each end of the well,

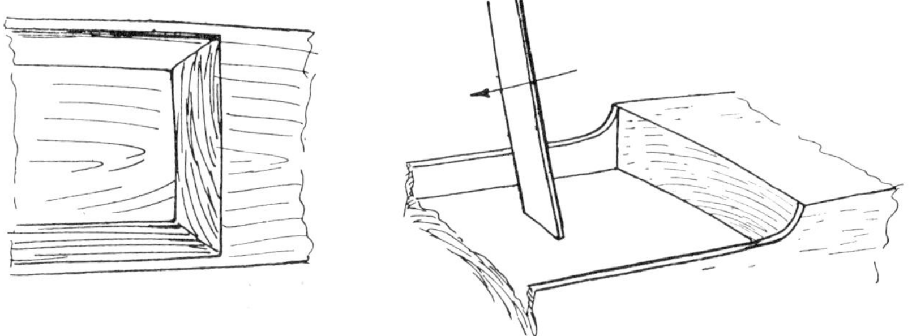

Fig. 23. Finishing the deck

leaving a little for the final finishing. Then cut along the sides, but not too closely, leaving the wood in the centre somewhat as shown in the sketch, Fig. 22. Then with a broad chisel remove the surplus wood in the centre. Great care is necessary to preserve the curve of the sheer—the depth should be equal throughout the length of the bulwarks—and at the same time to preserve the camber of the deck. When the depth is about correct the thickness of the sides should be reduced to approximately

$\frac{1}{16}$ in. and the bulkhead at the break of the poop and of the fo'c'sle should be finished off truly vertical. The recess at the break of the poop (see Fig. 14) should be carved out after the well deck is finished, blending the floor with the deck, and squaring up the sides. The surface of the deck should be scraped smooth and flat by means of a scraper, see Fig. 23. The scraper may be made from any hard steel—an old flat file or even a strip of hacksaw blade would do—which has been ground and stoned square across the end.

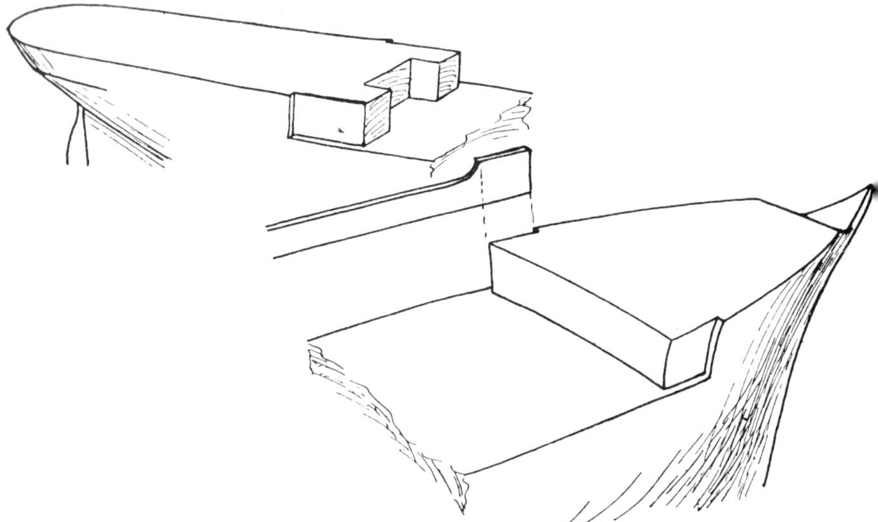

Fig. 24. Fitting the bulwarks separately

Fitting Bulwarks Separately

Those who prefer to fit the bulwarks separately should cut down the hull to the level of the deck. First mark on each side the level of the deck, as shown in the hull lines. Then cut away the wood until it is within $\frac{1}{16}$ in. of these lines, and finally produce the camber of the deck by cutting down to the lines on each side and leaving the centre untouched. Recesses should be cut on each side of the poop and fo'c'sle, as shown in Fig. 24, the depth of the recesses being made to suit the thickness of the material being used for the bulwarks. This may be of 1-mm. or $\frac{1}{16}$-in. plywood. In my *Cutty Sark* model I used $\frac{1}{16}$-in. satin walnut. The strips will be approximately 15 in. long by $\frac{1}{4}$ in. wide and should be curved to follow the sheer of the deck line. Some difficulty may be anticipated in persuading the strip to accommodate itself to the tumble-home amidships and the outward flare at station 16. The ends are, of course, controlled by being screwed and glued to the recesses. For the tumble-home amidships it will be necessary to make a block about 4 in. long by ¾ in. thick to fit between the bulwarks, having the sides sloped to the correct angle. Two clips, shaped as shown in Fig. 25, should next be made from plywood, having surfaces *A* cut to suit the tumble-home, and the recess *B* made sufficiently deep so that when the clips are pressed over the bulwarks, one at each end of the block, as shown in Fig. 25, the bulwarks are firmly clamped at the correct angle. If the bulwarks are thoroughly steamed before being finally glued and screwed in position,

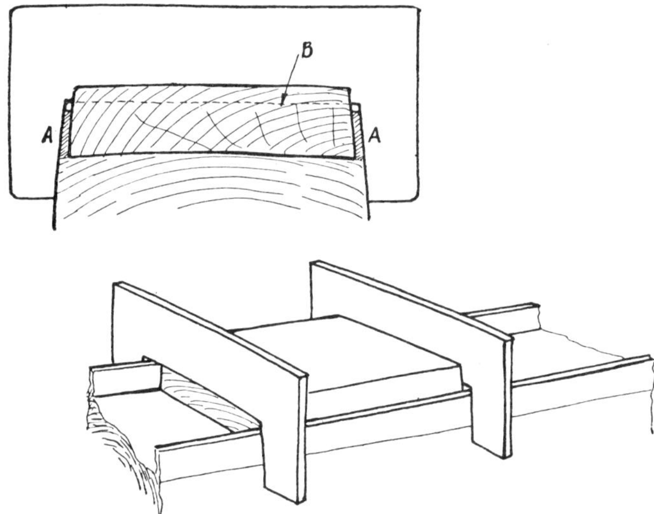

Fig. 25. Clips for setting bulwarks

and left clamped as described for say 24 hours, they will be found to be reasonably accurate when the clamps are removed. The outside of the bulwarks should be rubbed down perfectly smooth and flush with the sides of the hull before going any farther.

For a model with a bridge deck, the central structure may be left solid and the wells cut out fore and aft of it. On the other hand, if the bulwarks are to be fitted separately the deck should be cut out from the break of the poop to the fo'c's'le, which incidentally, will ensure the decks being in line with one another. The portion of the bulwarks in the way of the bridge deck will be raised to the height of the deck, and the structure itself built and decked over using ¹⁄₁₆ in. three-ply or thin close grained wood, such as sycamore. In some ships, e.g. *Wanderer*, Plate 3, and *Lyderhorn*, Plate 4, the raised portion of the bulwark at the bridge deck was curved inboard above the rail similar to the half round at the poop as shown in Fig. 2D, the rail line forming a continuous curve from end to end of the ship.

For a model with the bridge deck combined with the poop this should be left solid and covered over with Bristol board as already explained. The forward well deck should be cut out from the solid as it is scarcely worth while to fit separate bulwarks for the short length necessary.

Where the fo'c'sle head runs along to the figurehead, as in the *Rossshire* and *Sindia*, Fig. 3, and the *Lawhill*, Plate 5, and *Beatrice*, Plate 14, and many others, the bowsprit may be fixed by one of two methods. It may be bevelled to the correct angle and secured in place by a tiny screw and glue, or better still it may be inserted into a hole prepared for it. To facilitate the drilling of the hole extra material, as shown in Fig. 26, should be left before the final shaping of the fo'c'sle head, the foremost face being cut at right angles to the centre line of the bowsprit.

If sufficient material for this was not left in squaring up the block for the hull a block shaped as required may be pinned and glued in position. The surplus wood must be cut away or removed, as the case may be, after the drilling is completed satisfactorily.

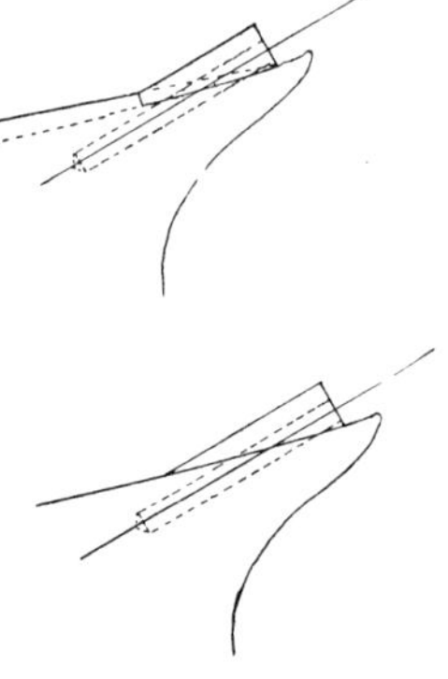

Fig. 26. **Drilling hole for bowsprit**

CHAPTER IV

MAIN DECK FITTINGS

FIG. 27 is a plan and elevation of the more important deck fittings, which is reproduced to the actual size for the model.

Covering the Decks

Assuming that the hull had been shaped as already described, the next thing is to cover the decks with Bristol board. This forms a smooth firm base on which to work, and with it there is no tendency for splinters to work up when fixing the rails, rigging, and deck details. Before fitting the decks, the bulkheads at the break of the poop and of the fo'c'sle should be covered with Bristol board. Figs. 28 and 29 give particulars of the portholes and doors or companion-ways in these. With reference to Fig. 28, in addition to the doors behind the stairs, there are doors on each side leading into the small extensions to the poop. That on the starboard side is the officers' W.C., and that on the port side, the officers' bathroom. It is easier to draw these on the Bristol board before fitting than after. The overlay covers the end grain of the wood, which is so difficult to hide when only paint is used. Bristol board is superior to any other cardboard, is very tough, and has a hard smooth surface. The correct thickness to use is two-sheet. Any art dealer supplies it.

Before covering the fo'c'sle head, the space between the two sets of houses or compartments underneath it should be cut away down to the level of the main deck. Although in the actual vessel this space extends to the stem, in the model it need only be cut about 1 in. forward of the bulkhead. A strip of card $\frac{1}{16}$ in. wide should be glued across the opening as shown in Fig. 29, to support the deck at this point.

In the *Archibald Russell* the forward deck house was the seamen's fo'c'sle, the space under the fo'c'sle head being used for sundry stores. This space was divided by an open space 16 ft. wide which accommodates the windlass. The hawse pipes lead into this space, and thus the water and mud from the anchor cables does not damage the stores which are kept in the lockers on either side. The windlass is located immediately below the capstan, and may be operated either by hand from the capstan, or by the donkey engine amidships through belts or ropes, for which guide pulleys are provided. There are two gear ratios in the drive from the capstan. The accommodation on the starboard side consists of the crew's bathroom—quite a luxury on a sailing ship— the hospital, bo'sun's stores, W.C., and a potato locker. On the port side we have the carpenter's shop, oil and lamp room, W.C., and the vegetable locker.

The outline of the Bristol board for covering the decks may be taken direct from the plan. The centre-line and the position of the more important fittings should be marked in pencil. In my opinion it is useless at this scale to attempt to draw lines to indicate the planking. They would be only 1/32 in. or less apart, and the only

Plate 20. **Main deck from roof of chart house**
—Archibald Russell

effect would be to mar the clean appearance of the decks. The extension which accommodates the standard compass will be noticed at the poop. This is supported at its forward end by the boat skid, which in turn, is provided with two iron supports. The photograph of this taken from the roof of the chart-house, Plate 20, will help to clear up many points in this region. The Bristol board for the poop and fo'c'sle head should be allowed to project very slightly all round. A strip of card should be cut as shown in the plan as a surround for both these decks. When these also are glued in position and properly set, the projecting edge should be smoothed very carefully with fine glass-paper to leave it projecting very slightly, but evenly all round.

In covering the main deck, a space $\frac{1}{16}$ in. wide should be left along each side just inside the bulwarks, to represent the water-ways. The card covering the recess at the poop and the space underneath the fo'c'sle head hould be fitted closely all round.

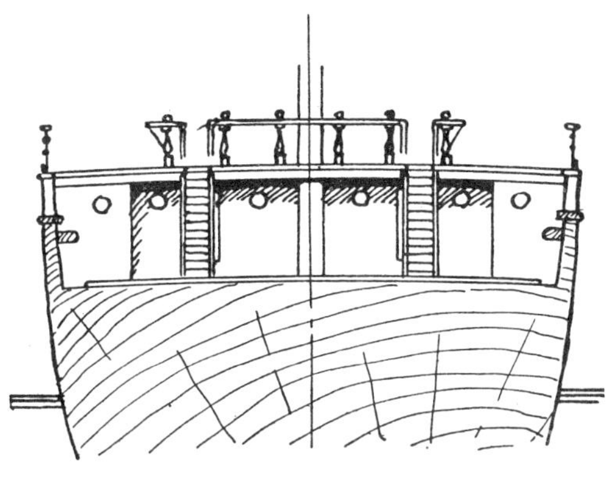

Fig. 28. Break of poop

Pin Rails and Eyes for Shrouds

Now that the bulwarks are finished, it is time to fit the pin rails. These are made from satin walnut or other close-grained wood, $\frac{1}{16}$-in. thick and approximately $13\frac{1}{4}$ in. long. For the most part the width is 5/64 in., but in the way of the shrouds the width is increased to $\frac{1}{8}$ in., as shown in the deck plan, Fig. 27.

Holes should be drilled as indicated in the sketch, Fig. 30, to take the eyes for the shrouds and backstays. There are five shrouds and nine backstays in each group. If the builder feels that fitting nine backstays is rather too much, three of them could be omitted and six holes drilled to occupy the space of nine. At this scale six backstays on each side for each mast will give quite a realistic effect. Details as to which may be omitted will be given later. In marking off for drilling, the pin rails should be fitted temporarily in place and the foremost holes in each group marked off opposite the centre-line of each mast, the remaining holes being marked off aft of these. With nine backstays their spacing will be a little closer than that for the shrouds. The dimensions on Fig. 30 should be adhered to.

The eyes for the shrouds and backstays are made from brass wire about 24-gauge thick (small domestic pins would do), cut into lengths of $\frac{5}{8}$ in. and formed into a loop at the centre, the ends being pushed through the rail and spread on the underside, as shown in Fig. 32. A strip of tape could be glued on the underside of the rail between the supports (see A, Fig. 31) to keep the eyes in position. These supports should be made from $\frac{1}{16}$-in. plywood or strip and glued in position just before the rail narrows, as shown in Fig. 31. They should

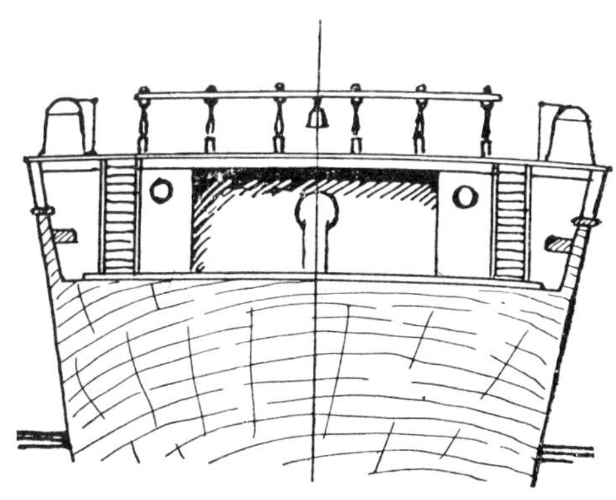

Fig. 29. Break of fo'c'sle

fit in the angle between the bulwark and the deck, and their upper surfaces should be 3/32 in. below the level of the rail in each case—twelve are required.

The pin rails should then be fitted and glued in place to rest on the supports and to lie snugly against the bulwarks along their entire length. To ensure this, small pieces of wood should be cut and wedged in position temporarily, as shown in Fig. 33. While the rails are held in this way they can be pressed down on to the tops of the supports and thus kept parallel with both the deck and the top-gallant rail. When I had got to this stage in my *Cutty Sark* model I laid the model on its side and put a fair amount of adhesive in the space between the brackets *A* (see Fig. 31) at each group of shrouds, and let it set. The other side was then treated similarly.

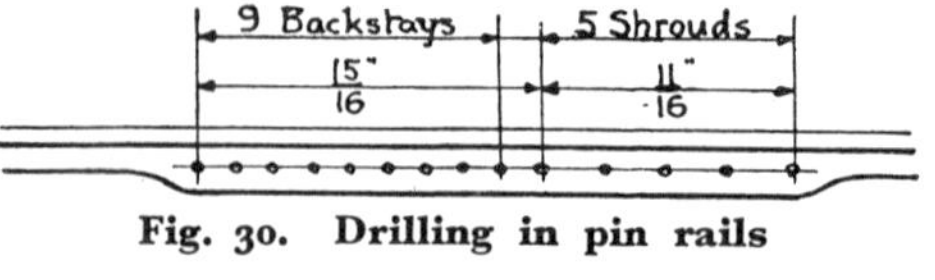

Fig. 30.   Drilling in pin rails

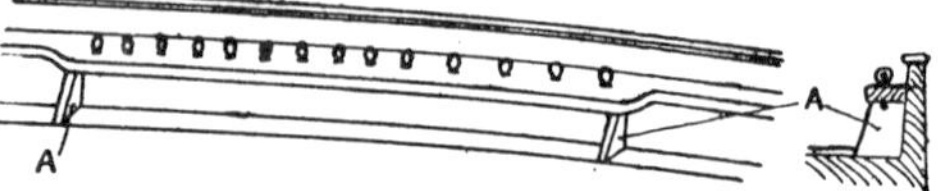

Fig. 31.   Pin rail supports

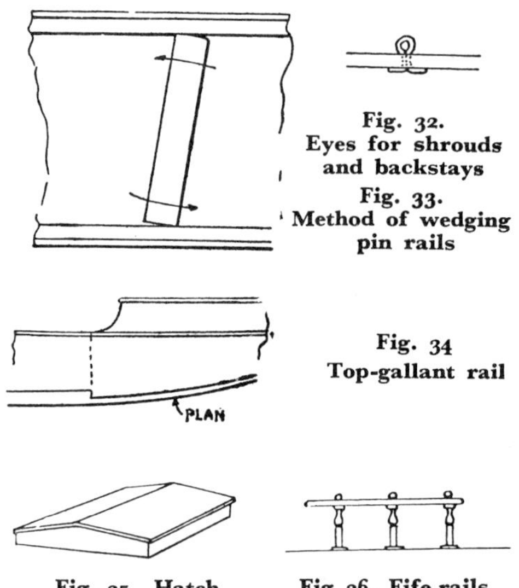

Fig. 32.
Eyes for shrouds
and backstays

Fig. 33.
Method of wedging
pin rails

Fig. 34
Top-gallant rail

Fig. 35. Hatch   Fig. 36. Fife rails

In this way the rail received extra support where the pull of the shrouds would come, and the eyes for the shrouds were secured against any tendency to pull out.

Top-gallant Rails

The top-gallant rails should next be fitted. They are made from Bristol board (thin Perspex might be used) cut to the outlines given on the plans in Fig. 27, the portion between the poop and the fo'c'sle being ⅛ in. wide, and the ends being reduced to about 1/16 in. wide. See Fig. 34. Great care will be necessary in cutting, but it is worth the trouble if each of the two pieces can be produced in one piece. The two pieces meet at the stem-head just above the scroll, whilst at the poop they are glued along the sides parallel with the poop deck. It should be noted that they do not follow the curve of the plating from the rail up to the poop and fo'c'sle-head ; the effect should be that shown in Fig. 34. When glued and set, the outer edge should be rubbed down with fine glass-paper until it projects only slightly beyond the ship's side, and on the poop and fo'c'sle there should be only about 1/32 in. of its width remaining, just enough to give the effect of a beading.

Hatches

The hatches are made of wood, shaped with a sloping top as shown in Fig. 35, the top being covered with Bristol board, which projects slightly all round. The fore hatch measures $\frac{3}{4}$ in. long by $\frac{5}{8}$ in. wide, the main hatch $1\frac{1}{4}$ in. long by $\frac{3}{4}$ in. wide, and the after hatch $\frac{3}{4}$ in. long by $\frac{9}{16}$ in. wide. The height in each case is 5/32 in. at the centre, sloping to $\frac{1}{8}$ in. at the sides. The separate hatch covers with their handles should not be shown, as the hatches are covered with a tarpaulin, unless when the hold is empty. When at sea the tarpaulin is secured by iron bars which are in turn fastened by wooden wedges driven into Z brackets riveted to the hatch covering. These may be seen in the photograph Plate 21 showing the break of the poop. The hatches should be glued to the main deck in the positions already marked out.

Fife Rails

For the fife rails in my *Cutty Sark* I was fortunate enough to find a thin plastic sheet, about 1/32 in. thick, which had fine linen as a base and was brown in colour. It had no tendency to split, and in its natural state it gave a very good representation of teak or mahogany, which was the wood used in the actual vessel. There is a variety of such materials in use nowadays, especially in aircraft construction. This was cut into strips $\frac{1}{16}$ in. wide, $\frac{3}{4}$ in. long, for the fore and main fife rails and $\frac{7}{8}$ in. long for the mizzen. From the plan it will be seen that the mizzen fife rails butt on to the half deck, and are thus square at their after ends. They should each be drilled for three pillars. The pillars could be made from ordinary pins, the heads forming the knobs which were formed in the actual pillars. The shape of the pillars below the rails could be suggested by using the insulation made for the wires in radio sets. Those who are expert with the lathe on miniature work might prefer to make them from brass rod, as shown in Fig. 36, the lower half of the pillars being left square.

Pumps

The pumps are situated between the mizzen fife rails, as shown in Fig. 27. A tiny block of wood $\frac{3}{16}$ in. by $\frac{1}{4}$ in. by $\frac{1}{8}$ in. high could be used to represent the pump body. The crankshaft, which need only be a straight piece of wire glued across the top of the fife rails, is provided with two flywheels made from card or thin plastic sheet. These are 7/32 in. diameter.

Half Deck

The half deck has three doors in its after end, that on the port side leading to the boys' quarters, the centre one to a companion way leading down to the 'tween decks, and that on the starboard side leading to the petty officers' quarters. The sills will be about 18 in. (or 3/32 in. in the model) above the deck to prevent the ingress of water when the decks are flooded by seas coming aboard. A block of wood should be prepared $\frac{15}{16}$ in. long by $1\frac{1}{16}$ in, wide by $\frac{7}{16}$ in. high. As with the chart house, it should be covered on the sides with paper and on the roof with thick Bristol board. The sides must be vertical and the base fitted to the slope and camber of the deck, as already explained in connection with the chart house. The railing which surrounds its roof, which will be seen in Plate 21, will be discussed later. A ladder to the roof and a rack for four

Plate 21. Break of poop—*Archibald Russell*

capstan bars are provided at its forward end. The dimensions and position for the small skylight on the roof may be taken direct from the drawing, Fig. 37.

Midship House

Having completed the chart house and the half deck, we should next tackle the midship house. The aftermost portion of this contains the donkey boiler and the steam winch. These need hardly concern us in our model as, when at sea, the double doors in the after side of the deckhouse would be closed. The only sign of their existence is the top of the boiler and the drums on the end of the shaft on each side of the house. These should be shown. The size and position of the top of the boiler, with its chimney, can be taken from the drawing, Fig. 27. The drums on the ends of the shaft may be used with or without the deck capstans in the general work of sailing the ship when the boiler is under steam, and for handling the cargo in places where no dock cranes are available. There is a grooved pulley on the inner side of the drum on the port side, which is used to drive the winch at the fore hatch and/or the windlass under the fo'c'sle head, as will be explained later.

The block of wood to represent the midship house will measure $1\frac{3}{16}$ in. long by $1\frac{1}{16}$ in. wide by $\frac{7}{16}$ in. high, and will be hollowed out on its underside to fit the deck, and curved on top to suit. As the deck, at this point, is practically level in a fore-and-aft direction, the ends will be at right-angles to the base and roof. Fig. 38 shows the position of the doors and portholes. At the after end there are two double doors, which could be painted or inked on the paper with which the sides are covered. At the forward end there is an iron ladder on the centre line, and a rack for four capstan bars on each side. The capstan bars could be represented by pieces of fine wire glued on, as could also the ladders, but it would be a finicky job and the result would hardly be worth the trouble. The simpler method of painting them on gives almost as good an effect at this scale. The hand rails on each side are more conspicuous, and should be represented by pieces of wire glued on, as already described for the chart house. The roof will be of Bristol board, three-sheet thick, projecting slightly all round.

Seamen's House

In the model this will measure $1\frac{1}{2}$ in. long by $1\frac{1}{16}$ in, wide by $\frac{7}{16}$ in. high and should be made in a similar manner to the other deck-houses. The deck slopes upwards slightly at this point, so the base and roof will be correspondingly sloped in relation to the ends. Fig. 39 shows the details of the sides and ends.

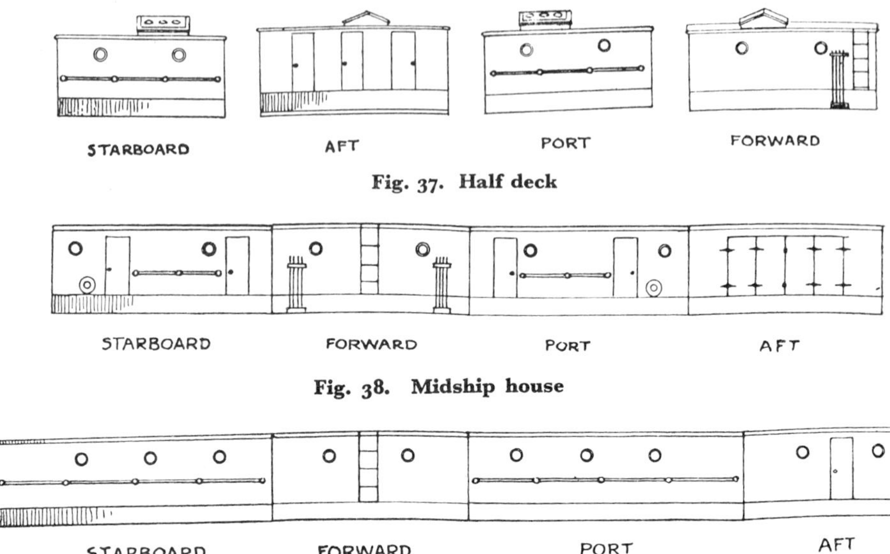

Fig. 37. **Half deck**

Fig. 38. **Midship house**

Fig. 39. **Seamen's house**

The deck-houses are painted white on the sides from the level of the sills of the doors upwards. Below this point they are painted dark-red or brown. The roofs will be of a brownish colour, a little darker than the shade used for the decks. The doors should be painted dark-brown to represent varnished wood. The lights in the portholes are 10 in. diameter and the brass frame 15 in. I have seen brass rings fitted around the portholes in a model to a scale of 1/32 in. to a foot, which is half the size of our model, so, if any of our modellers feel inclined, they could fit brass rings slightly larger than $\frac{1}{16}$ in. diameter driven into holes in the wood. The inside of the ring could be filled with Durofix or other transparent adhesive, to give the effect of glass.

The bulkheads at the break of the poop and of the fo'c'sle are painted white above the level of the sills, and dark-red or brown below, similar to the deck-houses. This will be seen in the photograph, Plate 21. The bulwarks are painted white on the insides, and the waterways dark-brown. The inside of the bulwarks should be painted before fixing the deck-houses in position, as otherwise the deck-houses get in the way.

For the benefit of the uninitiated we give a diagram (Fig. 40) of the *Archibald Russell* and her deck-houses, which is not to scale, but which will serve to explain the relative positions of the various deck erections, and also to amplify my remarks on the form of the deck-houses, viz. : that

the ends of the houses are vertical to the water line, and that their roofs
are parallel to the line of the deck. The roofs of the houses on the main
deck form, with the flying bridges, a continuous line from the poop to
the fo'c'sle head, the line being more or less parallel to the top-gallant
rail and the main deck. The beauty of the model will depend to a
considerable extent on the strict observance of these points, which are
inseparably bound up with the sheer line, the importance of which I have
already tried to emphasise.

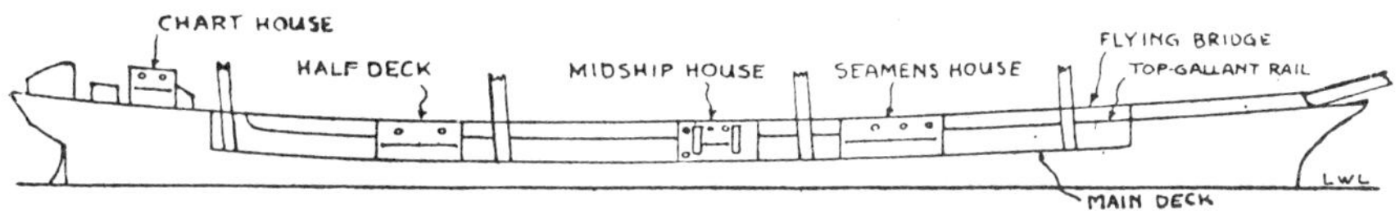

Fig. 40. Diagram of deckhouses

Lifeboats

The two lifeboats at the poop measure 24 ft. × 7 ft. × 3 ft.—or in
the model 1½ in. × $\frac{7}{16}$ in. × 7/32 in. The boats on the skids at the
midship house are, on the starboard side, a cutter 24 ft. × 6 ft. × 2 ft. 6 in.
(1½ in. × $\frac{3}{8}$ in. × say, $\frac{3}{16}$ in. in the model) and, on the port side, a gig
22 ft. × 5 ft. × 2 ft. (1$\frac{3}{8}$ in. × $\frac{5}{16}$ in. × say, 5/32 in. in the model). The
gig has a transom stern, whilst the others are double-ended. They should
be made from sycamore or other hard wood which has a close-grained
surface.

First cut a strip to the shape as shown in the section in Fig. 41, making
it the correct size for the lifeboats. Then shape the bow, being careful to
work to the drawing and to keep both sides alike. Next make a notch
at 1½ in. from the stem and cut away the wood until the stern is shaped,
taking care not to separate the boat until the form is almost complete.
When it is separated, the sternpost can be given the correct rake and
fineness. Note that the stem is rounded at the forefoot, whereas the
sternpost is straight and sloping throughout its length. If a piece of fine
wire is bent to form the keel, the stem and the sternpost, and glued in
position, it will improve the general effect. The ends of the wire should
be cut off just above the level of the boat cover. On completion, it will
be found that the sloping top of the strip has automatically produced the
sheer of the boat.

After the lifeboats have been finished the strip should be reduced to
suit the cutter, and after that is made it should be finally reduced for the
gig. Although this boat has a transom stern, the method of shaping it is
practically the same as for the others, except that the wire for the keel

need not be carried up the sternpost. In each case, the boats are left solid to represent the covers which are invariably fitted. If, however, the model is shown without sails, the gig could be hollowed out and tiny thwarts fitted.

A strip of Bristol board or 1/32-in. three-ply of about the width of the boat should be glued in position extending from one skid to the other, and at each end of this, chocks, made from the same material, and shaped to fit the underside of each boat, should be fitted. These may be seen in the photograph taken from the quay. (See Plate 26.)

Davits

These should be made from 18 or 20 s.w.g. brass wire, tapered toward the upper end if possible, and curved as shown in Fig. 42. The drawing also shows their positions. They should be pushed through holes in the pin rail close inside the bulwarks and into corresponding holes in the deck below. The photograph taken from the quay (see Plate 26) shows the blocks and tackle for lifting the boats, but at this small scale only the expert miniaturist would attempt them. They may, however, be suggested by fixing two eyes or hooks in each boat and a hook to the end of each of the davits, then secure a thread to the hook in the davit, lead it down to the eye in the boat, back to the hook in the davit, across to the curve of the davit and finally down to some convenient point in the pin rail. (See Fig. 42.)

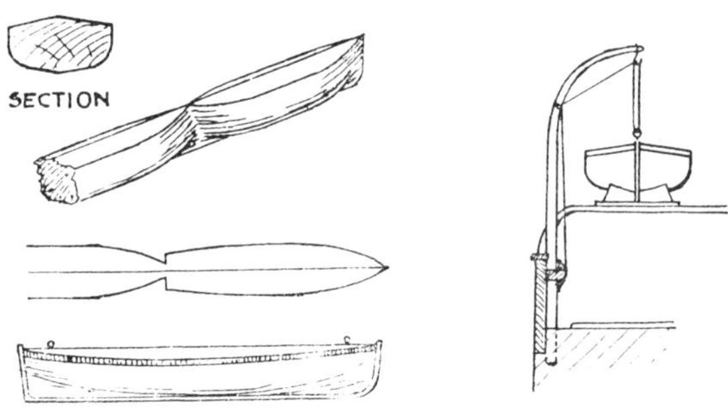

Fig. 41. Making lifeboats   Fig. 42. Rigging for davits

Skylights

There are four skylights in all, three of which have sloping tops and the fourth, that on the fo'c'sle head, has a flat top. They should be made of wood, shaped to suit, and covered with a piece of Bristol board which projects slightly all around to represent the hinged covers, see Fig. 43. Their positions and sizes are as follows :—

	Wide	Long	Lights		Panels
On roof of half deck ...	$\frac{1}{4}$ in.	$\frac{5}{16}$ in.	6	in	2
Midship house	9/32 in.	$\frac{7}{16}$ in.	8	,,	4
Seamen's house	9/32 in.	$\frac{7}{16}$ in.	8	,,	4
On fo'c'sle head	7/32 in.	7/32 in.	2	,,	I

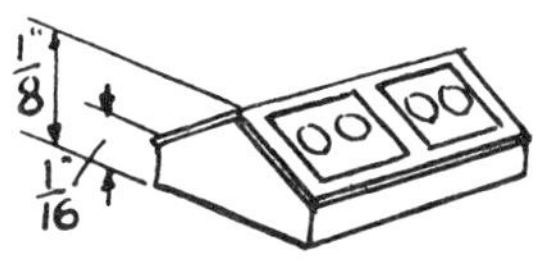

Fig. 43. Skylight

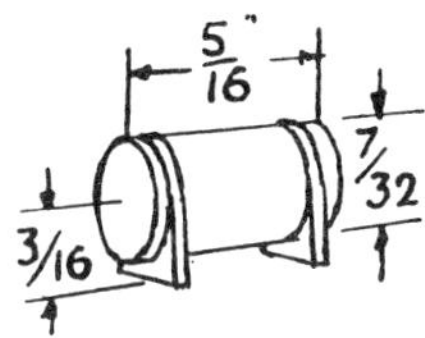

Fig. 44. Water tank

Those with sloping tops are $\frac{1}{16}$ in. high at the sides and $\frac{1}{8}$ in. high on the centre line. The remaining one is 3/32 in. high and should be cut to suit the slope of the fo'c'sle head. Holes about $\frac{1}{16}$ in. diameter should be cut in the Bristol board to represent the lights, and lines drawn to show the panelling. Their exact positions on their respective houses may be obtained from Fig. 27.

Donkey Boiler

The part of the boiler which is seen on the roof of the midship house is actually only a cover, the boiler proper being underneath with the chimney coming through it. When in use the chimney would probably have an extension piece fitted, but when at sea it would be of the length shown. This can best be represented in wood, $\frac{3}{8}$ in. diameter by $\frac{3}{16}$ in. high, rising to $\frac{1}{4}$ in. at the centre, with a piece of wire 14 or 16 s.w.g. for the chimney. The galley chimney may also be made of 16 s.w.g. wire, left full for the cowl and reduced below to represent the pipe.

Water Tank

In her earlier days the *Archibald Russell* had a rectangular water tank, 5 ft. by 4 ft. by 3 ft. 6 in. high on the roof of the midship house, but this has since been replaced by one of circular form about 5 ft. long. by 2 ft. 6 in. diameter. To make this, cut a piece of 7/32-in. dowelling $\frac{5}{16}$ in. long, mount it on two stands made of card or 1/32-in. plywood, and glue strips of paper over it and down the sides of the stands. For sketch, see Fig. 44. For its position, see plan, Fig. 27.

Capstans

These are six in number, five being on the main deck for the ordinary work of the ship and a larger one on the fo'c'sle head for handling the anchors. Their form and dimensions are given in Fig. 45, which is drawn twice the full size for the sake of clearness. The actual sizes may be seen in the drawings, Fig. 27. They should be turned in brass or hard wood. The expert miniaturist might drill holes for the capstan bars, but most of us would be content to indicate the holes with black paint. It will be noticed that the anchor capstan has a double row of holes, one row being used when in high gear and the other for low gear, the gears being arranged in the windlass on the main deck immediately below. The whelps on **the**

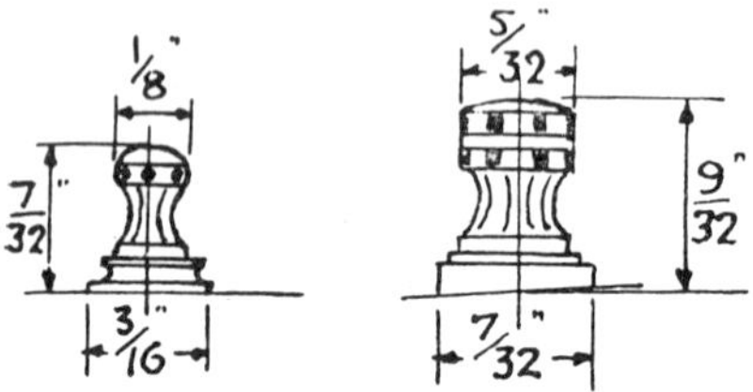

Fig. 45.   Capstans, twice full size

barrel of this capstan may be indicated either by lines drawn in black or by threads glued in position, or by fine wire soldered on if the capstan is turned from brass. An alternative method of making whelps for capstans is given on page 74 under " Capstans." The deck capstans should have short stems turned on the base for insertion into holes drilled in the main deck. The base of the anchor capstan, which may be a separate washer, should be sloped so that the capstan stands upright on the sloping deck.

Flying Bridges

The correct term is, I believe, Fore-and-Aft Gangways, and this describes their function, which is to enable the sailors to get along the ship in heavy weather when the decks may be flooded by seas coming aboard. To make them, take a strip of 1/32-in. ply-wood or the thin plastic sheet recommended for the fife rails, and cut it into strips $\frac{3}{16}$ in. wide, and of the lengths shown in Fig. 27. The two short bridges need no support in the centre, but the longer ones are each supported in three places. The diagrams Fig. 47 give the position of the stanchions in relation to the pillars for the hand rails. Opposite the hatches and fife rails there is only one stanchion under the bridges, but where the deck is clear there are two, one on each side of the gangway. They may be made from ordinary household pins with their heads cut off. They should be pressed into the deck by means of a jig as shown in Fig. 46. This is made from a piece of steel or brass about 10 s.w.g. or $\frac{1}{8}$ in. thick, shaped as shown. With this it is impossible to press the pins into the

deck at varying heights so long as it is pressed down to the deck every
time. The same piece may have a step cut at each of its four corners,
and thus may be used for other similar jobs about the model, e.g. the
poop rails and the rails around the fo'c'sle heads.

After fixing the stanchions, lay the strips for the gangways on top and
glue in position. Before doing so, however, the hand rails should be
fitted. The pillars—of fine wire—should be pressed into the strip as
near the edge as possible, using the above-mentioned jig. The hand
rails should be made of fine wire and soldered to the tops of the pillars.

Deck Winch

Besides driving the winch at the main hatch, the steam engine on the
Archibald Russell was arranged so that it could drive the windlass under
the fo'c'sle head. The part plan, Fig. 48, will help to explain how this
was done. Alongside the fife rail at the foremast a countershaft was
fitted, mounted in two bearings secured to the deck. It had a pulley on
each end, the outer one being in line with the pulley at the midship house
and the inner one being in line with a pulley on the windlass. These
pulleys were arranged for rope
drive. On the forward corner of
the midship house, and on both
corners of the seamen's house on
the port side, small guide pulleys
were fitted for the rope, the centres
of the larger pulleys being about
100 ft. apart. The drive was on
the low-geared side of the windlass,
so, presumably, was only used
for extra heavy lifts such as weigh-
ing the anchors from a deep
anchorage.

When I visited the ship in
1930 and 1931 this arrangement

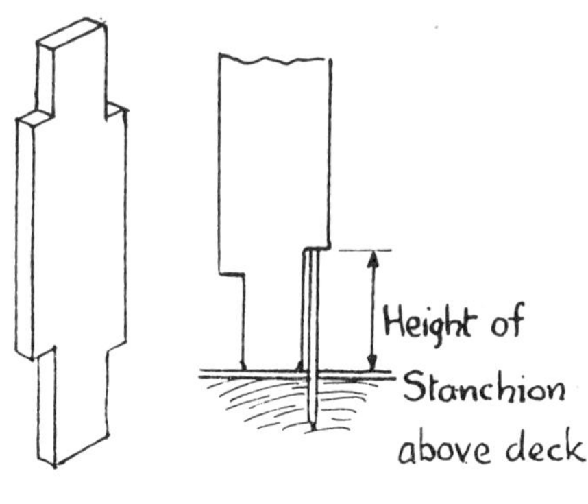

Fig. 46. Jig for stanchions

had been modified, the new scheme being as shown in Fig. 49. The
countershaft at the fife rails had been done away with and a small winch
provided just forward of the fore hatch. This was covered with a wooden
box when not in use, see Fig. 50. The shaft projected on each side, carrying
a warping drum at each end. These were probably used in connection
with the deck capstans for handling the fore braces and for heavy work
about the decks. From the upper photograph, see Plate 22, it would
appear that this winch was driven from the donkey engine by means

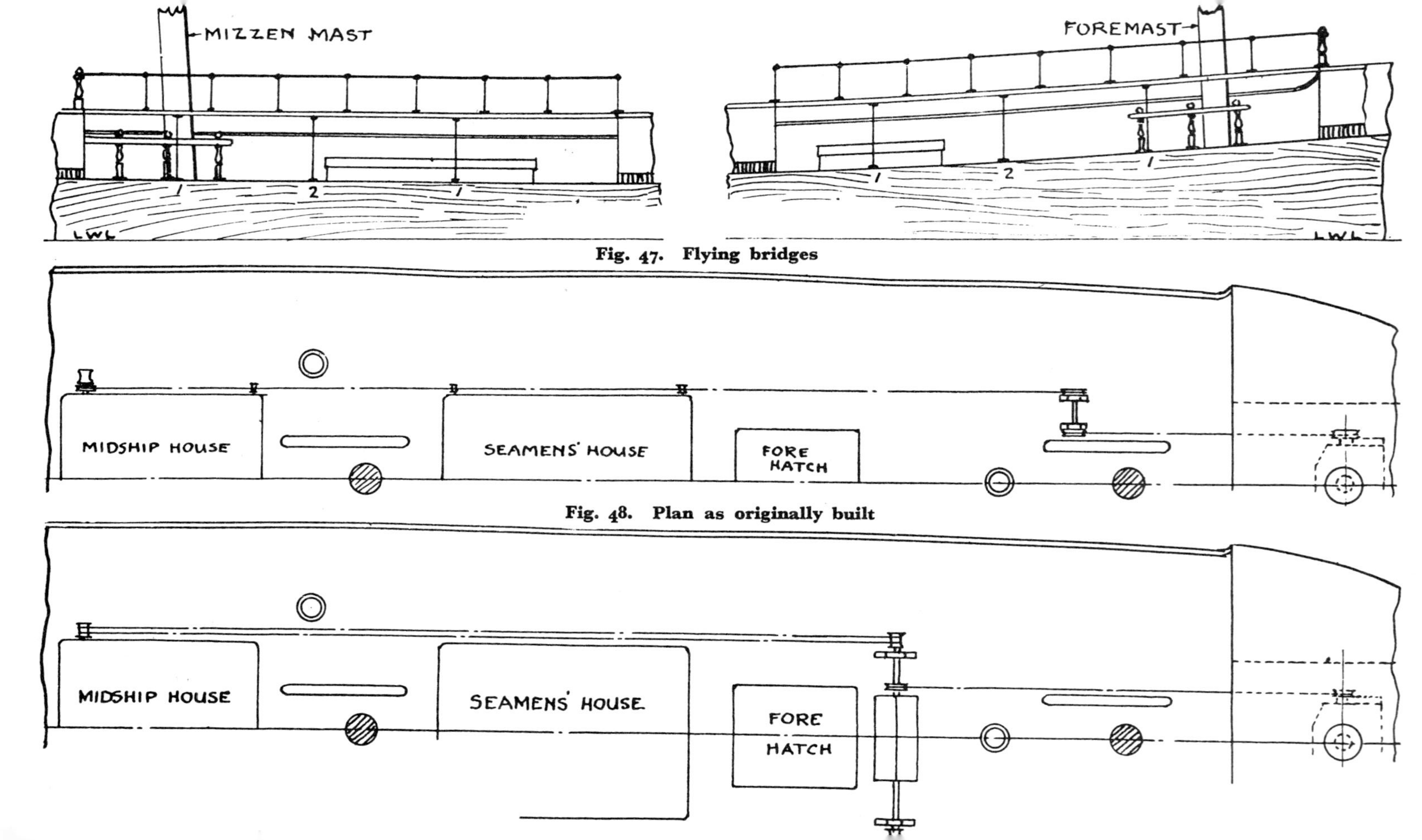

Fig. 47. Flying bridges

Fig. 48. Plan as originally built

of a flat belt from one drum to the other. On the inner side of the bearing and close to the wooden cover a rope pulley was provided for driving the windlass.

The constructor may follow either of these schemes according to whether he wishes to show the ship in her original or in her later state. The windlass need not be modelled, as it would be practically invisible. The winch at the fore hatch in its wooden cover could be shown as a solid block with a wire pushed through for the shaft. The drums could

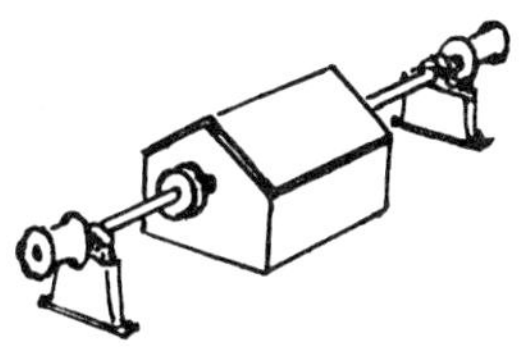

Fig. 50. Deck winch

be turned out of thick wire and the bearings made of wood $\frac{1}{16}$ in. or less in thickness. The guide pulleys on the houses could well be omitted.

In the view looking aft along the port side of the main deck (see Plate 22), the drum of the winch at the fore-hatch is shown in the foreground. The corresponding drum on the winch at the donkey engine can just be made out. The guide pulleys for the rope used in the earlier system may be seen on the corners of the seamen's house. I am not sure of the function of the uprights spaced along the sides of this house, but they were probably intended to protect the side of the house from being rubbed by the driving belt or rope from the donkey engine. The large pipes leading down to the fore-hatch are suction pipes for unloading the grain, and do not belong to the ship. The erection on the extreme right of the picture is the hen coop or the pigsty. This has occupied various positions during the career of the ship. The rack for capstan bars will be noticed, as also will the steps leading to the roof of the seamen's house.

In the view taken looking forward from the main hatch, Plate 23, the boiler casing and the water tank will be seen on the roof of the midship house. The skids for the boats and the cutter on the starboard side are also to be seen. The gig has been put overside from the chocks on the port side. The construction of the flying bridge can be gathered from the portion here shown, and also the single pillar alongside the hatch. The folding doors protecting the main winch, and the drums at each end of its shaft, are plainly shown.

Plate 22. The main deck looking aft, port side—*Archibald Russell*

Plate 23. Looking forward from main hatch—*Archibald Russell*

CHAPTER V

POOP FITTINGS

THE mechanism operating the rudder stock from the wheel of the *Archibald Russell* was not enclosed in the usual wooden case, the house evidently being considered a sufficient protection from the elements.   It is, however, too small to be modelled at our scale of $\frac{1}{16}$ in., so a plain block of wood $\frac{1}{4}$ in. cube should be glued in position on the poop deck, and the wheel pinned to its front face.   The wheel is located in the centre of the forward opening of the house and about 1 ft. ($\frac{1}{16}$ in.) aft of the forward edge.

In the model the wheel is $\frac{5}{16}$ in. diameter ove.. the rim and $\frac{3}{8}$ in. diameter over the tips of the handles.   It could be made from the plastic material already mentioned as being used for the fife rails.   I made a similar wheel for my *Cutty Sark* model, and found it very suitable for the job.   The house should be made from Bristol board, glued together at the corners.   Some may prefer to make it in tinplate and to solder it together.   The hand rail on each side can be glued or soldered together according to whether card or tin is used for making the house.   The shape of the house was given in Fig. 27, but is repeated here in a little more detail—see Fig. 51.   Incidentally, Figs. 51 to 55 are reproduced the actual size for the model.   The two lights in the roof—see Fig. 27 aforementioned—could be glazed with cellophane.   Gratings 5/32 in. square are placed one on each side of the wheel.   These could be made of wood or card marked with rows of dots to suggest the grating.

In a large number of four-mast barques the wheel was in the open, without protection of any kind.   This affords an opportunity for a very nice piece of modelling of which full use should be made.   The open wheel of one of the later vessels, the *Viking*, may be seen in Plate 24.   The casing containing the gear, was usually made of teak or mahogany, varnished, and the name of the ship was painted on the side panels. For the model this should be carved from a piece of walnut or dark wood. The four pillars supporting the casing were sometimes elaborately turned and could be represented by tiny beads threaded on the wires which support the casing.   The rudder stock comes up from below, and should be shown.   Gratings were usually arranged on each side to form seats.

In the *Viking* the wheel shown is the emergency wheel, the main wheel being amidships. The long casing in the foreground, which is also repeated on the starboard side, covers the steering chains from the mid-

Plate 24. Wheel of " Viking "
Note: *The principal wheel was amidships*

ships wheel which are connected to the tiller on the rudder stock. These casings must always be represented in the model of a vessel with the main steering wheels situated amidships—which is invariably the case with a ship having a bridge deck, whether combined with the poop or separate. For the earlier four-mast barques with an open wheel on the poop there would be no chain casings, but otherwise the wheel would be similar to the one here shown.

Cabin Skylight

This was of the usual barrel-top type and should be carved from a block of close-grained wood—dark walnut would be suitable. In the actual ship it was made of mahogany or teak and the wood was left in its natural colour, being merely oiled or varnished. The shape and size may be taken from the sketch, Fig. 52.

Chart House

In some ships this was built of teak or mahogany and was nicely framed and panelled. In the *Archibald Russell*, however, it was made of steel, as was more usual at the time she was built. The particulars are given in Fig. 53. It contains a table and racks for the charts and signal flags, and also a settee. A companion leads to the accommodation below. For the model, cut a piece of wood $\frac{9}{16}$ in. long by $\frac{5}{8}$ in. wide by $\frac{7}{16}$ in. high. The four sides should be vertical, so the base and roof will not be exactly at right-angles to the ends, as the base must follow the slope of the poop, and the roof should be parallel to it. The base must also be fitted to the camber of the poop deck and the roof must have a camber similar to that of the deck. It is advisable to cover the sides with paper and to paint the doors and portholes on it. The portholes could be holes cut in the

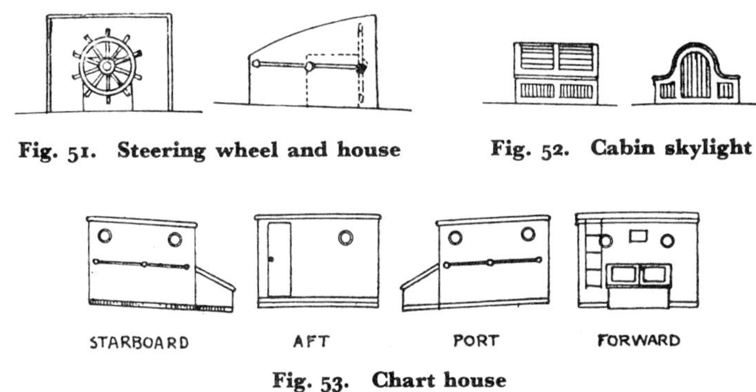

Fig. 51. **Steering wheel and house**   Fig. 52. **Cabin skylight**

Fig. 53. **Chart house**

paper, and are approximately $\frac{1}{16}$ in. in diameter. Note that the sill of the door is about 6 in. above the level of the deck—1/32 in. at our scale. Rails are fitted along each side ; these may be represented by a piece of wire glued on after fixing the paper sides. A ladder to the roof is provided at the forward end of the chart house on the starboard side. The roof should be of Bristol board, not less than three-sheet thick, and should project slightly all round. The small rectangle on the forward side of the chart house, see Plate 27, is the bulder's name-plate. This will be seen in the photograph, the more prominent words being Scotts and Greenock. A small locker with a sloping roof is situated immediately forward of the chart house. This should be represented by a suitably shaped block of wood, glued in position, and covered with a projecting sheet of Bristol board. Ventilators are fitted on each side, but they need hardly be shown in a model of this size.

Meat Safe

In the plan, Fig. 27, the small rectangle just abaft the jigger mast is the meat safe. The details of this may be seen in the photograph of the

Fig. 54.
Standard
compass

Fig. 55.
Bollards

control platform. Plate 25. Its dimensions in the model are ¼ in. by ⅛ in. by ¼ in. high. It was made of mahogany or teak, but if modelled in this material the grain would be too obvious. Nature can't be scaled! Better to make it of dark walnut or sycamore—in the latter case it must be stained or painted brown. The projecting top could be made of 1/32-in. three-ply and the slats suggested by lines drawn or painted in Indian ink. The gripes for securing it to the deck could be omitted.

Binnacle

The helmsman's binnacle was situated immediately aft of the skylight, as shown in the plan—Fig. 27. Its height above the deck is 4 ft. 6 in. (9/32 in.) and the diameter of the column is approximately 16 in. (3/32 in.) Its general form may be taken from that seen in the photograph of the control platform, Plate 25, with which it was similar, except that it was not mounted on a platform. It should be made from a piece of hardwood fixed to a square of Bristol board. A hole should be drilled through it near the top and a piece of fine wire pushed through with a small bead threaded on at each end and fixed in position with a spot of Durofix—see Fig. 54. If desired, the angle brackets below the beads could be made of Bristol board.

Standard Compass

This is exactly the same as the helmsman's compass already described. The stand which supports it will be seen in the photograph. Plate 25. In the model it measures ¼ in. square by 3/32 in. high. It should be made from a piece of 1/32-in. or 1-mm. three-ply and supported by small pegs or beads at the corners—see Fig. 54.

Bollards

These are made by pressing two pins through a piece of Bristol board ¼ in. long by 3/32 in. wide. The pins should be glued in position with the heads projecting 3/32 in. above the surface. When set, the points are cut off $\frac{1}{16}$ in. below the surface—see Fig. 55. Two small holes are then drilled in the deck at the correct position, when the bollards may be pressed down and glued in place. Twelve bollards are required : three pairs for the main deck, two for the fo'c'sle head, and one for the poop. Their exact positions are indicated in the plan, Fig. 27.

Ventilators

Six ventilators are required, three on the poop, one just aft of the pumps, one on the roof of the midships house, and the sixth on the roof of the seamen's house. A seventh is fitted just under the break of the fo'c'sle, but as it is somewhat hidden by the spare anchor, it may be omitted if desired. They may be made from close-grained wood, which is first cut into a strip of the section shown in Fig. 56. This is then formed into the cowl and the pipe as shown in the sketch. The ventilators on the poop have pipes 8 in. and 12 in. diameter, say $\frac{1}{16}$ in. on the model. The remaining three have pipes 18 in. and 20 in. diameter, or, say 3/32 in. on the model, their various heights being as shown in Fig. 27. They should be made about $\frac{1}{8}$ in. longer than shown, and pushed into holes drilled in the deck and in the roof of the houses, as shown in the plan.

Flagstaff

The fitting between the wheel-house and the taffrail, shown in the plan, Fig. 27, is a socket for the flagstaff. The flagstaff is only used when the vessel is entering or actually in a port, as it gets in the way of the spanker boom, so I suggest we omit it in the model.

Eyes for Jigger Mast Shrouds

These are similar to those already provided for the remaining three masts—see Fig. 32—except that they cannot be spread out underneath and must be pressed firmly enough into the deck to resist the pull of the shrouds. They can be made of fine wire—24 gauge or somewhat smaller— cut into $\frac{1}{2}$-in. lengths and formed into a loop at the centre. Tiny holes should be drilled in the poop deck in the positions shown in Fig. 57 and the eyes tipped with Durofix and pressed in. It will be noticed that in this vessel the foremost shrouds for the jigger mast are not fixed in line with the centre of the mast as is usually the case. This is probably necessitated by the position of the quarter boats.

In connection with the jigger mast shrouds it should be noted that in vessels with the poop rails at the side the shrouds are secured inside the rail, whereas when the vessel has a half-round at the poop the shrouds are fixed at its lower edge where it joins the bulwark strake and outside

Plate 25. The control platform and standard compass, as seen from the poop
—Archibald Russell

Plate 26. Side of the hull of the " Archibald Russell," from the quay

the rails. This is because the shrouds must be fixed to the side plating to ensure sufficient strength for the anchorage.

Quarter Boat Skids

In the photograph, see Plate 26, showing the outside of the hull, as seen from the dockside, which is reproduced herewith, the boat skids for the quarter boats will be noticed. These also support the forward edge of the control platform. They should be made from a piece of copper wire about 20 s.w.g., the ends being bent over and, when fitting, pressed into holes drilled in the rails. Before fitting in place, two pieces of similar

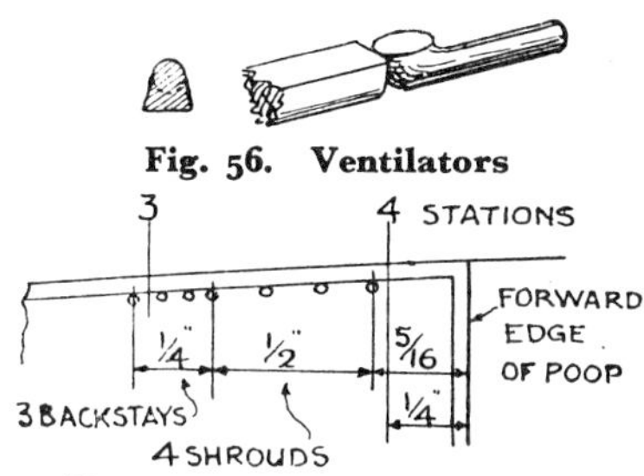

Fig. 56. Ventilators

Fig. 57. Position of eyebolts

wire should be soldered on at right-angles to form supports for the control platform, as shown in the photograph of the break of the poop—see Plate 21. These should fit into holes drilled in the deck. When fitting, care must be taken to ensure that the wire supports the control platform at its correct level. Durofix could be used to attach the platform to the wire.

There are still a number of deck fittings to be made and the builder will perhaps find this part of the job a trifle dull and tedious. However, he should remember that it is the deck details which give character to a ship model. Moreover, to the man who knows the ship, accuracy in the deck details gives that personal touch which raises the model from being merely the model of any ship, into being a replica of the particular ship which he has known and loved.

Companion Ladders

The companion ladders from the poop and the fo'c'sle head next claim our attention. These are four in number, and as they are all alike, it may be worth our while to make a jig for spacing the steps. This is made from a strip of wood about $\frac{1}{16}$ in. thick by $\frac{1}{4}$ in. or more in width. On one side mark out a triangle to the dimensions given. This will give us the correct slope for the steps. Nine notches should be cut $\frac{1}{16}$ in. deep and parallel with the horizontal line and all equally spaced at approximately $\frac{1}{16}$ in. pitch. A fine fretsaw will be necessary. Before finally cutting the notches, nine scores should be cut in the edge as a preliminary; otherwise the saw will slip on the sloping edge and it will be difficult to space them evenly. For the steps, cut a long strip of Bristol board $\frac{1}{16}$ in. wide and

cut it into equal lengths of 5/32 in. each. Lay nine of these pieces, one
in each notch, in the jig. The sides of the ladders should be made from
the same strip and should be cut a little longer than necessary. Take a
pair of sides and cover the inside surfaces with a liberal application of
Durofix or other adhesive. Press them on to the ends of the steps and
hold in position a little while until set. When quite dry, remove the
assembly from the jig and trim the ends to the dimensions given in the
sketch, Fig. 58. They may now be fitted and glued in their respective
positions on the model.

Railings

The railings at the break of the fo'c'sle, those around the half-deck,
and those around the control platform, should next be made. In the
ship these are heavy wooden railings and are supported by turned wooden
posts having a square base and a round knob above the rail. They may
be seen in the photographs, and their size and shape may be taken
direct from the plan Fig. 27. They are very similar to the fife rails
and the method for making these, described on page 51, should be
followed. From Fig. 28 it will be seen that the pillars nearest the boats
support only short lengths of rail, the sloping lines being iron stays to
support the outer ends. The rail between the two centre posts should

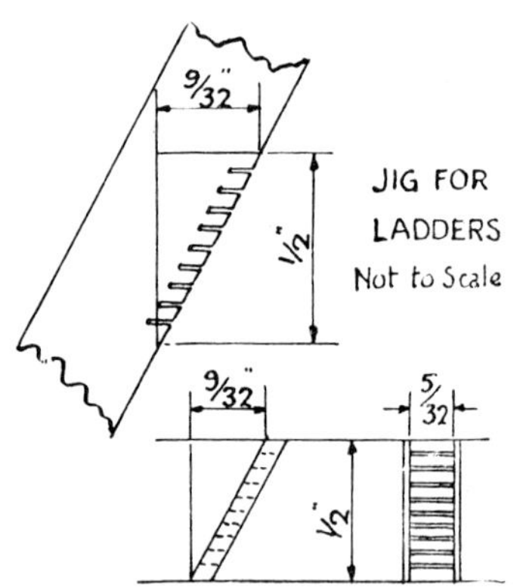

Fig. 58. Companion ladders

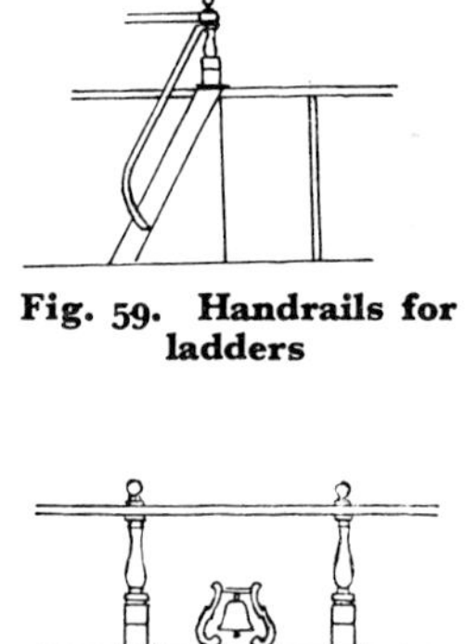

Fig. 59. Handrails for ladders

Fig. 60. Bell and mounting

be omitted, leaving a gap which gives access to the flying bridge (see
Plate 21). The rail around the platform thus consists of two L-shaped
pieces, each supported by four posts. At the companion ladders, short
pieces of wire could be glued to the underside of the rail and the sides of
the ladders for hand rails, as shown in Fig. 59.

The rails around the roof of the half-deck are in two portions, having gaps on the forward and after sides to give access to the flying bridges. The rail across the break of the fo'c'sle is as shown in Fig. 29. In that drawing the bell is shown hanging from the rail, whereas it should have been shown hanging from a bracket fixed to the deck, as shown in Fig. 60. Hand rails may be fitted to the companion ladders, as already described for the poop.

The rails around the outside of the poop and fo'c'sle head should be made at a later stage. Otherwise they are liable to be damaged, and, moreover, those around the poop would interfere with the fitting of the jigger-mast shrouds. See page 91.

Fire Buckets

Twelve fire buckets, six on each side, are located on the control platform, as may be seen from the upper photograph on page 68, but as they are so tiny they could well be omitted.

Harness Casks

A couple of harness casks were placed under the break of the poop

Plate 27. The poop from corner of half deck—*Archibald Russell*

and may be seen in the photograph, Plate 21. These are from 3 ft. to 3 ft. 6 in. high—almost ¼ in. in the model—and could be turned from brass wire 10 s.w.g., or ⅛-in. wooden dowel. The advantage of using brass is that they can be painted in such a way as to leaye narrow bright strips to represent the polished brass hoops by which the actual casks were bound.

The photograph, Plate 27, shows the poop taken from the corner of the roof of the half-deck. On the left one may see the chocks for the lifeboats with their connecting platform, also the gripes for securing the boat. In the centre one can just make out the row of fire buckets, six on each side of the control platform, placed in a rack at the foot of the pillars for the railing. Another view of these may be seen in the photograph of the break of the poop, Plate 21. On the extreme right the hinge for lifting up the flying bridge may be seen, also the attachment of the rope to the hand rail. Aft of it is the standard compass, and still farther aft, the base of the jigger mast with its spider band and the cleats for the brails of the spanker.

CHAPTER VI

FORECASTLE FITTINGS

THE railing along the after edge of the fo'c'sle head is similar to that at the break of the poop and, as will be seen from Fig. 29, its length is equal to the space between the companion ladders. The bell underneath it has been described already—see Fig. 60. The remainder of the railings should be added after the lower masts are erected, and the forestay fitted, see page 92. The bollards are similar to those on the main deck. Two smaller pairs are situated just inside the rails as shown on the plan, Fig. 27. The short rail for belaying pins is similar to the fife rails, and the method described for making them should be used here. The skylight and the capstan have been described already.

Capstan

When discussing capstans recently with Mr. Tilley, one of the Bristol Ship Model Club members, he explained to me the method he has employed for fixing the whelps on the barrel of the capstan for a model cabin cruiser which he is making. This was to bind a length of fine brass wire axially along the capstan, taking it a sufficient number of times around to suit the number of whelps required—see A, Fig. 61. The wire is then pressed in close to the " waist " of the capstan (see B) and the whole dipped into a bath of solder. The larger diameters marked A, on Fig. 61C, are then finished in the lathe, cutting away the wire and leaving the lengths representing the whelps securely soldered in position. The capstan he showed me certainly proved the soundness of the scheme.

Lighthouses

These can be turned from brass or hard wood, the height above deck being $\frac{1}{4}$ in., and the diameter at the base $\frac{3}{16}$ in. The shape is shown in Fig. 27, mentioned above. They should have a stem turned on the base for fitting into holes which must be drilled on each side of the deck in the appropriate places. If made of wood a small slit should be cut on the forward side of each and a strip of tin inserted to represent the reflector. If the lighthouses are made of brass these strips can be soldered in position.

73

The lighthouses are painted white, and the reflectors red for the port side and green for the starboard. A glass bead could be inserted in the lighthouse alongside the reflector to represent the lamp.

Anchors

There are two anchors on the fo'c'sle head and a spare one at the break of the fo'c'sle. Their size may be taken from the plan, Fig. 27, and their general shape, of the flukes, at least, from the photograph of the spare anchor, Plate 28, on page 75. In this photograph the stock is seen lashed to the shank of the anchor. The ball on the upper end of the stock, not seen in the photograph, is screwed on. When fitting the stock the ball is screwed off and the stock is then pushed through the eye in the

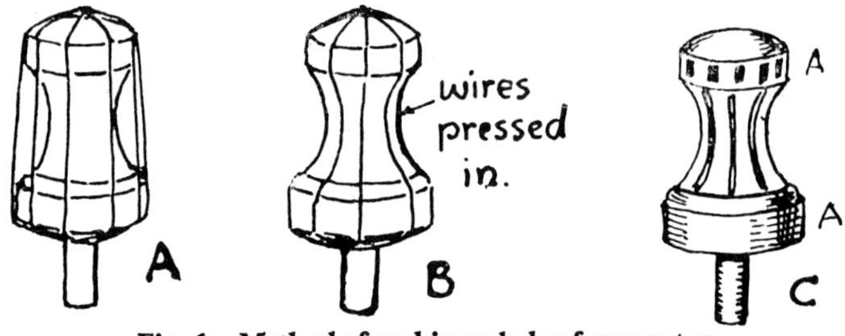

Fig. 61. Method of making whelps for capstan

shank and secured in position against its shoulder by the cotter seen in the photograph. The anchor rests on a shaped wooden block and is secured by chains to eyebolts in the deck. How much of this is reproduced in the model depends on the skill and patience of the modeller.

The anchors on the fo'c'sle head may have their stocks in position ready for use, especially if the model is shown without sails. Otherwise they may be lashed on the fo'c'sle head alongside the shanks of the anchors, which was the usual position for them when at sea. In the model the stocks will be about $\frac{5}{8}$ in. long. The band around the middle of the shank was fitted with a shackle for use when getting the anchor inboard. The anchor may be cut out of metal or even Perspex. The palms of the flukes will be about $\frac{1}{8}$ in. long by 3/32 in. wide, and should be soldered or cemented in position. In large anchors the ring at the head of the shank was often replaced by a shackle secured with a pin through the shank.

Catheads

These should be made of wire or hard wood—split bamboo is very suitable—about $\frac{1}{16}$ in. square. They slope outwards and upwards, and their position may be taken from the plan, Fig. 27. The inner end of each should be rounded to fit into holes drilled in the sides of the hull. If they are pushed into the holes with Durofix the surplus expelled from the hole can be formed into a fillet under the catheads.

Anchor Crane

The anchor crane consists of a stout pillar, a strut which is forked to rest on the base of the pillar, and a tie to support the strut at its outer end. The lengths and relative diameters should be taken from Fig. 27. The crane should be made in wire of the appropriate thicknesses, soldered at the joints, and with the pillar left long enough to fit into a hole in the

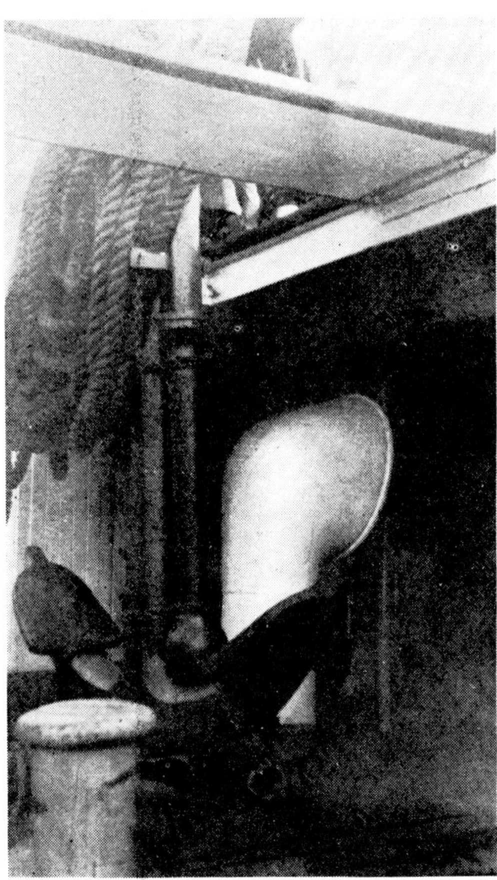

Plate 28. Spare anchor at break of fo'c'sle—*Archibald Russell*

fo'c'sle head. The lower block of the tackle, which had triple sheaved blocks, is lashed to the strut when not in use.

Before the introduction of the anchor crane, davits for handling the anchors were fitted on each side of the fo'c'sle head. These will be seen in the photograph of the *Beatrice*, Plate 14. Previous to the introduction of davits the anchors were handled by a heavy tackle which was suspended by a pendant from the fore-topmast head. This may be seen in the photograph of the *Jordanhill*, Plate 12, which had neither crane nor davits for the anchors. With the introduction of the anchor crane the catheads became less necessary and in some ships they were dispensed with altogether. In the deck plan of *Herzogin Cecilie*, Fig. 3, it will be seen that she had none. In the *Lawhill* the catheads were steel tees as will be seen in Plate 34.

CHAPTER VII

EXTERIOR DETAILS OF THE HULL

BEFORE the hull may be considered complete, there are a few exterior details to be attended to, and one of the most important of these is the scroll, which, in this vessel, replaces the more usual figurehead. This is shown in some detail in Fig. 62. It will be seen that the decoration blends with the line of the plating, and when the ship had painted ports the dark band above emphasised the effect. Later, as was the case with most ships of the period, the decoration was removed, leaving merely the termination of the scroll. Unfortunately, whoever removed the decoration paid no attention to the form, cutting it off opposite the point marked *A* in the drawing, and thus leaving the crude effect shown in the accompanying photograph, Plate 29. This was very kindly sent me by Mr. Donald Middleton, of Northampton, who visited the ship when she was moored at Goole during the war. However, as we are showing the ship with painted ports, we should show the decoration in its original form. To do this, the strip which forms the top-gallant rail—see Fig. 34—should terminate at about the point marked *B*, in Fig. 62, and be continued by a more or less triangular sheet of brass of the same thickness pinned or screwed to the wood below. The tip should be turned down to form the scroll and a blob of solder sweated on the bend and filed to a point as shown, The fullness below, marked *C* in the drawing, could be built up with Durofix. The scroll on each side may be formed from a wisp of silk or cotton thread fixed in place with adhesive. With a little careful manipulation with a pointed tool, this can be persuaded to lie correctly before the adhesive sets. After painting the hull the decoration should be gilded, when it will look quite effective.

Rudder

Fig. 63 shows the rudder in full detail as actually fitted to the ship. How much of this detail is shown must be left to the discretion and to the ability of the modeller. The important point to remember, whether much or little detail is shown, is that the centre-line of the rudder stock must be in line with the centre-line of the hinge pins.

Bumkins

These are short metal arms—in the early ships they were short booms known as boomkins—standing out from the ship's side to take the anchorage for the standing ends of the brace tackles. In the later sailing ships they were fixed to the sheer strake just below the rail and hinged so as not to be in the way when docking the ship. The pull of the braces was taken by a short chain which led aft, and was secured to the ship's plating. There were three bumkins on each side and their position may be taken from the hull drawing, Fig. 27. In our model they may be represented by domestic pins pressed in the hull in their respective positions, and cut off at $\frac{1}{8}$ in. or $\frac{3}{16}$ in. from the side. At our scale the chain could well be ignored.

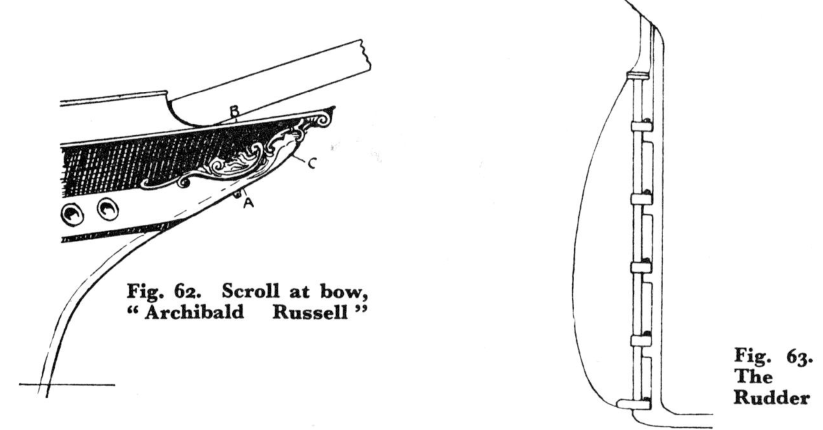

Fig. 62. Scroll at bow, " Archibald Russell "

Fig. 63. The Rudder

Freeing Ports

There are five freeing ports on each side of the main-deck bulwarks. They are hinged horizontally at the centre and again at the upper edge, so as to allow the doors to swing outwards, and so free the deck of water when any comes aboard. Their position is indicated in Fig. 27, and their appearance may be seen in the photograph, Plate 26. The mooring ports—three on each side—are also shown in the same drawings and photograph. These should be drilled and then elongated with a small round file. The freeing ports, however, could be shown by merely cutting the outline with a small chisel, making the cut sufficiently deep to show through the painting.

Portholes

The portholes should be shown by drilling $\frac{1}{16}$-in. holes in the appropriate positions and putting a spot of Durofix in each to represent the glazing.

Alternatively, they could be painted, using black or dark green, and if a suitable punch is available they could be marked in before painting as with the freeing ports. I have seen portholes shown very effectively by inserting a tiny brass ring in each hole, but this would not be appropriate here as the frames do not show on the outside. This will be seen in the photograph already referred to.

Bilge Keels

The *Archibald Russell* was probably the only four-masted barque to be fitted with bilge keels. I have no information as to the effect they produced, although I expect they would help considerably to steady the vessel in a seaway. But as she was one of the last large sailing ships to be built in Britain the question as to whether her successors would be similarly fitted did not arise. Bilge keels usually consisted of a bulb section plate 1 ft. or more in depth secured to the hull plating by an angle on each side. They were situated at the curve of the bilge on each side of the ship, and extended for about half its length or even more, being equidistant from each end. They could be represented in our model by strips of split bamboo or perspex or even by a strip of tin glued into a narrow slot cut along the hull. At the small scale of our model the angles could be ignored.

Plate 29. Scroll at bow " Archibald Russell," 1935

Painting

The hull above the row of ports and up to the top-gallant rail is painted black, as is also the narrow strip below the ports. The ports themselves are black on a white ground. The upper edge of the port band follows the lower edge of the upper strake of plating, which is shown clearly in the photograph of the hull, Plate 26. The lower edge of the narrow black band below the ports follows the lower edge of the second strake of plating, which is shown also in the same photograph. The black band should be 1/32 in. wide in the model, becoming slightly wider towards the stem. Under the counter the line of the plating rises somewhat, and the black band follows it until it meets the upper strake, as shown in Fig. 64. Above the top-gallant rail the hull is painted white. At the stern, from the point where the top-gallant rail ends—see Fig. 27—the white terminates in an upward curve as shown in Fig. 64.

Below the narrow black band the hull is painted light-grey with perhaps a slight tendency to purple—but much more grey than purple. From the water-line downwards the hull is coated with anti-fouling paint, which is approximately Indian-red in colour. Note that the painted water-line is slightly above the actual L.W.L., rising somewhat towards each end of the vessel. The name on the bows and stern should be in yellow letters, and the Port of Registry on the stern should be Glasgow, to agree with the period represented in our model. The name at the bows is painted just below the top-gallant rail and extends from just below the lighthouses to halfway along the top-gallant fo'c'sle. With regard to the kind of paint to use, my experience favours ordinary oil colours, artist's quality. If the finishing coat is used with a little megilp it will

Fig. 64. Painting at stern

be found that varnish is unnecessary. Varnish should be avoided if possible, as it tends to clog fine detail, besides which it gives an unnatural glossiness to the work.

At the end of the 19th century and early in the 20th, the scheme of colouring with painted ports as described for the *Archibald Russell* was by far the most popular among shipowners. Painted ports were popular from the 1870's onward, but at that time the grey below the port strake had not been introduced, the usual scheme being to paint the hull black from the port strake to the waterline. In other words, the hull was painted black from the waterline, or boot-topping, to the rail, with a white strake on which the ports were painted. Usually the ports were shown touching the upper edge of the white strake with a narrow white space below, but in some cases they were joined to the lower edge with the white space above. *Fascadale*, Plate 17, is a case in point. *Armadale*, *Carradale*, and other Dale liners had the ports painted in this way, but the scheme was adopted by very few owners. In any case the normal scheme with the ports touching the upper edge of the white strake was more reminiscent of the naval wooden walls and the East Indiamen from which the idea was taken.

Some owners had their ships painted white, and when this was combined with a fine-lined hull and a tall sail plan the effect was very yacht like. The famous three skysail yarder *Queen Margaret* and the well-known ships of the Sierra line had white hulls and were noted for their beauty and smartness. American ships were usually painted black. Quite a number of ship owners painted the bulwark strake and sometimes the next lower strake black and below that grey to the boot topping. *Lyderhorn*, Plate 4, illustrates this scheme as does also the ship seen behind *Mount Stewart* in Plate 31. *Lyderhorn* had, in addition, a white line 4 in. to 6 in. wide painted along the upper edge of the lower strake which emphasised the curve of the sheer line. The model of the *Pass of Melfort*, in the Science Museum, is an example of a four-mast barque with only the bulwark strake painted black. *Jordanhill*, Plate 12, shows yet another scheme of colouring, a grey hull with a 4 in. to 6 in. white line along the sheer strake. It must be realised, however, that the painting of the same ship varied from time to time, either due to a change of ownership or a change of master, or, in some cases, due to other causes. The *Archibald Russell* for example, in addition to the painted ports shown in Plate 18, was later painted white and, later again, black. The sides of the poop, whether a half-round or a flat plate, the sides of the topgallant fo'c'sle, and the plates above the normal line of the bulwarks at the bridge deck, were usually painted white.

Note on Figureheads

This seems to be an appropriate time for a discussion on figureheads. Many otherwise fine models are spoilt by an awkward figurehead. Perhaps the fact that so few of us have had the opportunity or privilege of seeing a really fine figurehead has something to do with it. At its best the figurehead was a dream of beauty in the way it blended with, and finalised, the lines of the bows and stem. Some of the small sailing coasters had rather quaint figureheads, but these had been carved by such craftsmen as were available at the small ship-yards. Those who carved the figureheads of the clippers and the larger ships and barques, were usually artists famous at their craft, and took their work very seriously.

Apart from the difficulty most amateurs find in drawing or carving— especially in carving—the human figure, the principal fault in most of the figureheads one sees on ship models is that they are too stiff and straight. The figure seems to have been carved for the normal upright pose and then fixed in position in line with the stem of the model. The result is that the figure is in a rather awkward and uncomfortable position with its eyes staring down into the sea. The figurehead should be shown looking forward in the direction in which the vessel is sailing. Whilst the lower portion of the figure slopes in line with the stem, the chest and shoulders are arched back to carry the head in an upright position.

The photographs, Plates 30 to 35, are given as typical examples. The earliest is the figurehead of H.M.S. *Sapphire*, of 1858, Plate 30. In these early ships the stem was more upright than in later ships, consequently the general line of the figure is more upright. This is a very good example of the way the scroll in the sheer line of the ship is blended with the draperies of the figurehead. This feature was discussed in the " Ship Modellers' Corner," in the issue of *The Model Engineer* for August 31st, 1944.

The next example, Plate 31, is from the ship *Mount Stewart*, built in Aberdeen in 1891, and shows the use of a male figure as a figurehead. At this time it was the custom for the figure to have one arm extended backward and the other flexed across the chest. The draperies are still blended with the scroll of the sheer line. The decorated panel above the sheer line tapering down from the draperies, is very characteristic of this period. When painted ports were abandoned this panel often disappeared. Something of the kind happened with the *Archibald Russell*. This photograph of the *Mount Stewart* illustrates also what we have been saying about the painting of the *Archibald Russell*, the only difference being that the *Mount Stewart* had a beading along the sheer line above the ports, whereas the *Archibald Russell* had none.

Plate 32 shows the figurehead of the *Killoran*, a big three-mast barque, built at Troon, in 1900. Originally she had painted ports and most probably the draperies of the figurehead were continued in a scroll. At the time the photograph was taken this had disappeared, but still the figurehead fits the stem and the head is thrown back so that the whole figure, is straining forward with the ship.

The figurehead of the *Beatrice*, Plate 33, was renowned for its beauty. The lines on the bows leading up to its draperies serve to emphasise the graceful blend of figurehead and ship. The photograph of the *Lawhill*,

Plate 30. Figurehead of
H.M.S. " Sapphire "

Plate 34, shows another fine example of one of the later figureheads. The scroll in the draperies was probably moulded into the sheer line when the ship was built. The figurehead of the *Port Jackson*, Plate 35, is a typical example of the earlier four-mast barques. The rich decoration in the panel below is reminiscent of that on the clipper ships, and of the more spacious days before the economies of this utilitarian age had begun to make themselves felt.

As a final comment on this point, we add an outline drawing, Fig. 65, traced from the builder's plans of the *Archibald Russell*, showing the figurehead fitted to her sister ship, *Hougomont*. The draperies are blended very artistically with the sheer line and the scroll which is formed above it.

In conclusion, the point to bear in mind when fitting a figurehead to a ship model, is that, whatever the angle of the stem, the figure should be fitted gracefully to it, and that the head and shoulders are always arranged so that the eyes are looking forward. In some cases the figure was shown with an outstretched arm, sometimes holding a trumpet, and in the well-known case of the *Cutty Sark*, whose figurehead represented the witch, Nannie, the left arm reached out to grasp the tail of Tam o' Shanter's grey mare, Meg.

Fig. 65. Figurehead of the four-masted barque " Hougomont "
Traced from builder's plan

Plate 31. Bow and figurehead of " Mount Stewart "

Plate 32. Figurehead of "Killoran"

Plate 33. Bow and figurehead of "Beatrice"

Photo by R. M. Cookson

Plate 34.   Bow and figurehead of "Lawhill"

Plate 35.   Figurehead of "Port Jackson"

CHAPTER VIII

RIGGING

HAVING completed the hull and its fittings, we are now ready to start on the rigging. First come the masts. In the *Archibald Russell* the fore, main and mizzen masts are in three sections, whilst the jigger mast is in two. Many of the ships of the period had the jigger mast made as one tapering steel tube, while the three remaining masts were in two pieces, the lower and topmasts forming one piece and the top-gallant and royal masts forming the other. However, the masts of the *Archibald Russell* were made on the older plan.

For the lower masts, the topmasts and the bowsprit, I would recommend the wooden knitting needles which used to be obtainable at Woolworths and may still be on the market. They were made of hard wood, and if care is taken in their selection, good straight-grained wood will be found. For the lower masts and the bowsprit use 5/32 in. diameter pins (No. oo), and for the jigger mast and the topmasts use ⅛ in. diameter (No. 10). For the top-gallant masts and the jigger topmast split bamboo or sycamore is very useful. Split bamboo in particular is very strong, and takes on a high degree of finish. Incidentally, this is a very useful material for the ship modeller. It was brought to my notice a few years ago by one of the Bristol Ship Model Club members. He used it extensively in miniature modelling, and as I was interested, he brought me a bundle of 100 lengths about ⅛ in. square by 18 in. long. They are sold to gardeners, who use them for marking young plants. They are evidently made from large bamboo sticks, and their length is controlled by the distance between the joints. As sold, one side is the natural hard surface of the bamboo, and this feature may often be turned to advantage. It can be split very easily into long parallel strips of almost unlimited fineness.

The drawing Fig. 66 gives the lengths of the masts and the position of the various fittings. The fact that the foremast is shorter than the main or mizzen, is due to the curvature of the deck as it follows the sheer line. The mast tops are at the same height above the water-line, as also are the crosstrees and the trucks. This uniformity in the masts was considered an ugly feature when it was first introduced, but it became practically universal, mainly because it made the masts and yards interchangeable. This was sometimes useful in an emergency, and was economical for both the builders and the owners.

The Lower Masts

To commence with the lower masts. In the jigger mast the portion from the underside of the mast top to the mast cap should be reduced in diameter to 3/32 in. and below this, flats to this diameter should be made on each side of the mast for the cheeks. The cheeks, see Fig. 67, should be cut out of Bristol board and glued on each side of the mast. Along the upper edge of these fix the trestle trees, short pieces of wood $\frac{1}{16}$ in. deep by 1/32 in. thick. These support the crosstrees, which may be of wire or split bamboo 1/32 in. square by $\frac{5}{8}$ in. long. These are glued in position, one forward and one aft of the lower mast.

The tops for the other masts are somewhat larger than that for the jigger mast. First the mast should be reduced to $\frac{1}{8}$ in. diameter, as shown in Fig. 68, with flats on each side similar to those for the jigger mast. The cheeks should be glued in position, after which the top itself can be threaded over the mast-head until it rests on the cheeks and on the step or shoulder made by reducing the mast in diameter. Fig. 68 gives the shape and size for the top, which should be made from the thin reinforced plastic material already recommended for the wheel and fife rails. Failing this, it may be made from very thin three-ply. The larger of the holes should be a close fit on the $\frac{1}{8}$ in. diameter mast-head. The smaller hole, $\frac{1}{16}$ in. diameter, is for the foot of the topmast. The rectangular holes on each side should be made sufficiently large to clear the shrouds.

The Bowsprit

The bowsprit should next be made, using the 5/32 in. diameter material already mentioned. The length is given in Fig. 69, as are also the diameters to which it should be tapered. The hole for receiving the bowsprit should be a good fit for the spar, but if there should be any difficulty in drilling it at the correct angle, the hole could be opened out and the angle adjusted when fitting the shrouds and bobstay. Similarly with the masts, I have found it convenient to have the hole slightly larger than the mast—only a very little, of course—and then to line up the masts by means of the shrouds and stays. Still, it is advisable to go to some little trouble when drilling the holes for the masts and bowsprit. A jig or template may be made to get the correct rake, and when drilling the holes a friend should be called in to see that the drill lies true with the centre-line of the ship.

Shrouds and Stays

Some model makers like to prepare all the " bits and pieces " before they start the assembly ; but in the case of rigging a ship model I find it more interesting to fit the parts as they are made. An actual ship, during all the various stages of the rigging operations, is intensely interesting to study, and, personally, I find the same kind of interest in watching the progress of a model as it is being rigged.

Before we step the lower masts the shrouds and stays should be prepared. The shrouds are made of black linen thread and should be cut into 11-in. lengths. Four lengths are required for the jigger mast and five each for the remaining three masts. Each length should be folded in the middle and an eye $\frac{1}{4}$ in. long formed by binding the loop with fine Silko. The fifth length, for the fore, main and mizzen masts, should have an eye splice, but in a model of this scale it is scarcely necessary. The stays also are made of black linen thread. All four are double and each has an eye approximately $\frac{5}{8}$ in. long at the centre, similar to those in the shrouds. They are also seized together at some little distance above the deck, but this seizing should be added after fitting the stay, when it serves to taughten it.

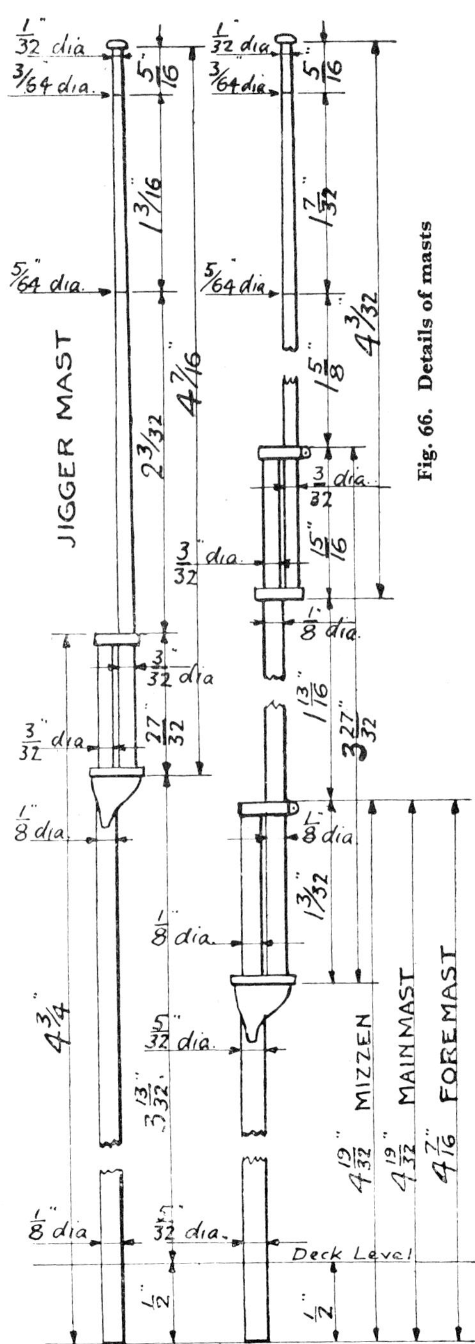

Fig. 66. Details of masts

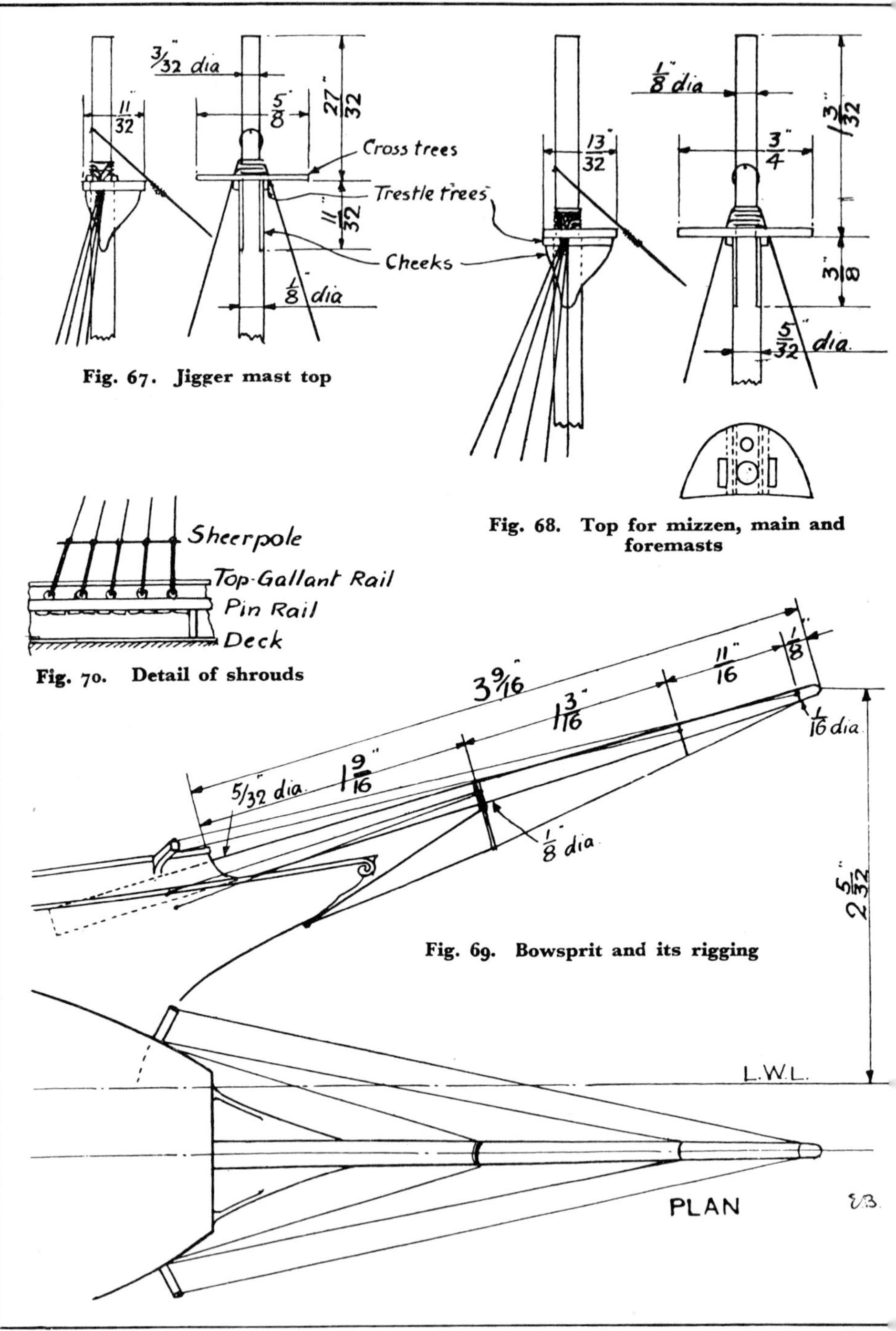

Fig. 67. Jigger mast top

Fig. 68. Top for mizzen, main and foremasts

Fig. 70. Detail of shrouds

Fig. 69. Bowsprit and its rigging

Erection of Lower Masts

We are now ready to erect the masts. It is best to work from aft forward. Insert the jigger mast in its hole after having put some Durofix on the base of the mast. Loop a pair of shrouds over the mast-head and bring them down on the starboard side through the hole provided in the mast top. Tie them temporarily to the two forward eyes on the poop. Repeat the process on the port side. The next pair will come down on the starboard side and be tied to the third and fourth of the eyes provided. The fourth pair are fitted similarly on the port side. Now tighten the shrouds, pulling the mast to one side or the other until it is plumb and true when viewed from forward or aft. The rake, when viewed from the side, should be a little more than the correct figure, so that when the stay is drawn tight it corrects it, at the same time tightening the shrouds. The correct figure for the rake of each mast, taking them in order from aft forward, is $1\frac{1}{8}$ in., 1 in., $\frac{7}{8}$ in. and $\frac{3}{4}$ in. per foot. The stay should next be slipped over the mast-head and the two lower ends fixed to the deck between the mizzen fife rails $\frac{1}{4}$ in. or so apart and $\frac{1}{4}$ in. forward of the C.L. of the mizzen mast. The neatest way to fix them is to make a hole at the correct position with a fine bradawl (I use a shoemaker's awl), then sharpen a small stick to a point, press this point on to the thread while holding it tight, and press the thread into the hole, the point of the stick having first been dipped into Durofix. A slight sidewards movement of the stick breaks off the point, leaving it in the hole with the thread. When the adhesive is thoroughly dry, the stick can be trimmed flush, thus making a fastening at once secure and neat. I believe this was the sailor's method when he made his models aboard ship. Having fixed both ends of the stay, a seizing should be put on a little aft of the mizzen mast, drawing them together and thus further tightening them. To prevent the stay slipping down the masthead, a tiny pin should be inserted for the loop to rest on, and a spot of adhesive will make it secure. A touch of adhesive should also be put on the seizings, on both the stay and the shrouds, and on the knots where the shrouds are tied to the eyes,

To finish the shrouds, apart from the ratlines which are fitted later, (see page 109) the sheer pole should be fitted. This should be of thin wire—24 s.w.g. or less—and may be glued to the shrouds as shown in Fig. 70. The ends of the shrouds should then be tied to the sheer pole. A smear of adhesive should be put on each of the shrouds and the two threads squeezed together to represent the bottle-screw, the knot representing the eye where the shroud is shackled to the screw.

The procedure for the mizzen, main, and foremasts is exactly the same, except that they have five shrouds on each side instead of four.

The extra shroud should be made in one piece for both sides, taking a turn round the mast-head and bringing down one end on either side. The lower ends of the stays are secured on each side of the mast as for the jigger mast stay, except that they are fixed in line with the C.L. of the mast between the fife rails instead of forward of it. The forestay should be secured below the pin rail at the forward edge of the fo'c'stle-head and so arranged as to clear the post of the anchor crane.

We reproduce in Plate 36 a photograph of the *Cutty Sark* model described in *The Model Engineer* for March 4th, 1943, when it was at the stage which we have now reached with the *Archibald Russell*. The comparison should be helpful. The *Cutty Sark* model is to the same scale and made in the same manner as this present model. It will be noticed that I fitted only four shrouds per side on each mast instead of the actual five ; also, that the forestay has no seizing at its lower end as with the *Archibald Russell*. With regard to the forestay, the same difference is to be found in the actual vessels.

Rigging Plan

We include herewith a rigging plan with key of the *Archibald Russell*, Fig. 71, showing the standing rigging and the braces. The lead of the halliards from the mast to the deck is not shown, but will be given in due course. The upper shrouds are omitted on the fore, mizzen, and jigger masts, for the sake of clearness. The drawing is exactly half the size of the model.

Erection of Bowsprit

We can now proceed with the rigging of the bowsprit. To secure the martingale or dolphin-striker, cut out a small piece of brass or tin 3/32 in. × ½ in., rounding the ends and bending it to encircle the bowsprit at the middle jib stay. The ends will come together with sufficient space left between them to receive the wire bobstay. The inner surfaces should be tinned. Next make the bobstay, using brass or copper wire about 24 s.w.g. Make this long enough to include the martingale and to allow of the other end being inserted into a hole in the stem ; 1¼ in. will do nicely. Make a sharp bend in the wire 9/32 in. from one end to form the martingale, and tin it at the bend. Then pierce a small hole in the stem a little below the scroll, as shown in Fig. 72, to receive the inner end of the bobstay. Insert the bowsprit in the hull, thread on the clip, press the bobstay into the hole in the stem, and bring the other end to fit between the ends of the clip, as shown in Fig. 72. With a suitable bolster in one hand and the soldering iron in the other, press the clip together so as to

1. jn, mizzen and jigger
2. opgallant stay
3. in and mizzen royal stay
4. nker boom topping lift
5. ,, gaff ,, ,,
6. igs
7. nker sheet
8. e, mast and mizzen brace
9. e, mast and mizzen lower topsail brace
10. e, main and mizzen upper topsail brace
11.
12. e, main and mizzen lower topgallant brace
13.

61. Fore, main and mizzen upper topgallant brace
62. Fore, main and mizzen royal brace
63. Fore, main and mizzen upper topsail halliard
64. Fore, main and mizzen upper topgallant sail (for " t'gan'l ") halliard
65. Fore, main and mizzen royal halliard
66. Flag halliards
67. Ensign halliards

Plate 36. A model of the " Cutty Sark " during rigging

sweat the ends to the wire between. A soldering iron is safer than a
blowpipe when soldering clips which encircle wooden spars, as it does
not burn the wood. Now drill a fine hole horizontally through the clip
and the bowsprit, and a second hole for the fore-topmast stay—see
Fig. 71. Insert a fine wire in each hole, allowing them to project about
1/32 in. on either side. The bowsprit shrouds, which are actually made
of chain, but may be represented by linen thread in a model of the size of
ours, should be looped and glued over the ends of the wire at the clip and
fixed to the hull just below and forward of the catheads in the manner
already described for the mast stays. The alignment of the bowsprit
should be checked and corrected if necessary when fitting the shrouds.
The remaining rigging for the bowsprit should be left until the fore-
topmast is fitted.

Topmasts

The fore-, main- and mizzen-topmasts may be made separately from the top-gallant masts, as shown in Fig. 66, or, can be made in one piece, see Fig. 75 and page 102 the space between them at the doubling being represented by a hollow on each side. At the lower end of the doubling the hollow is actually cut away for a depth of $\frac{1}{8}$ in. to clear the shrouds. This will be found to simplify construction and erection, and the effect is practically the same as when they are built separately. However, as we may have some sticklers for absolute accuracy amongst our readers, I will try to describe both methods.

To make the topmasts separately, cut off three lengths to the dimensions given in Fig. 66, and reduce them at the upper ends for the length of the doubling. The lower end should be reduced to $\frac{1}{16}$ in. diameter for a length of 1/32 in., to fit the hole in the lower mast top. To represent the trestle trees, cut out a rectangular piece of fibre or three-ply to the dimensions given in Fig. 73A. This is then slipped over the upper end of the topmast to rest on the shoulder made by reducing its diameter. Next make a clip for the mast cap, using a strip of brass or tin, 3/32 in. wide by $\frac{1}{8}$ in. long, rounded at the ends and bent to the shape shown in Fig. 73B, leaving a space between the ends to receive a wire clip for the yards. The ends should be tinned on the inner faces so that they can be soldered to the yard clip before fitting in position. This clip is a piece of wire, 24 s.w.g. by $\frac{7}{8}$ in. long, bent to form a vee and tinned at the angle. A similar but somewhat larger clip should be made for the lower mast cap, using a strip 3/32 in. wide by $\frac{11}{16}$ in. long, and, for the yard clip, a piece of wire about 1 in. long.

Erection

To erect the topmasts, first fix the larger clip to the lower mast-head, inserting between it and the mast-head on the after side a piece of cord, 8 in. long, for the top-gallant stay (51), also looping over the top of the mast two 10-in. lengths for the lower mast backstays (38). Next put the foot of the topmast through the clip at the cap and between the encircling loop of the mast stay, inserting the $\frac{1}{16}$ in. diameter portion into the hole prepared for it in the mast

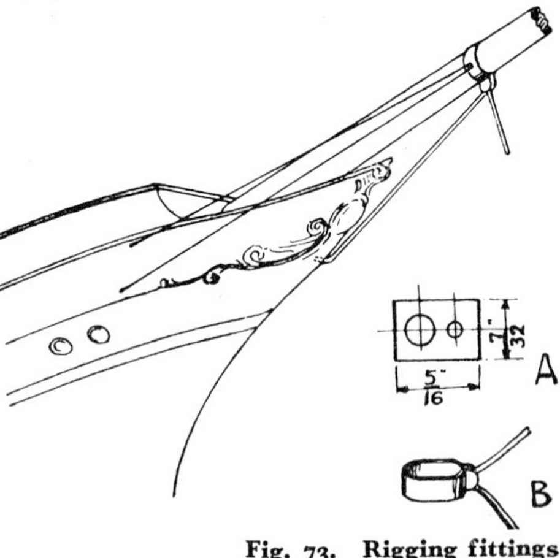

Fig. 72. **Bowsprit shrouds and bobstay**

Fig. 73. **Rigging fittings**

top. Insert the wire yard clip between the ends of the mast clip and solder them together. To tighten the clip, press the sides into the space between the mast, as shown in Fig. 64, taking care to have the top mast parallel to the lower mast. Now fit the crosstrees, on top of the plate, which represents the trestle-trees, one on the after side of the mast and one forward of it. These should be of wire, 24 gauge by $\frac{9}{16}$ in. and $\frac{5}{8}$ in. long, bent at the ends, as shown in Fig. 74.

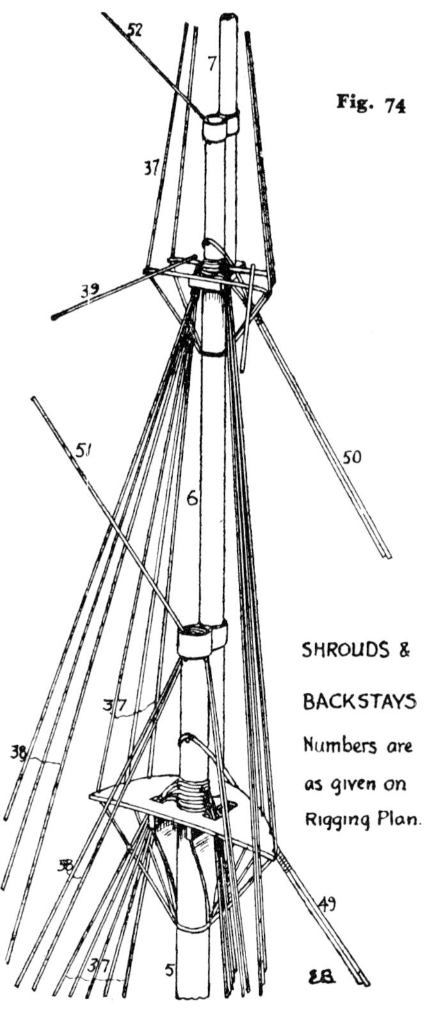

Shrouds

The topmast shrouds (37), should next be fitted. There are three on each side and they are fitted in the same manner and order as were those for the lower masts, except that there is only one pair and one single on each side. The lower ends should be continued downward to form the futtock shrouds, being brought over the edge of the mast top, which is notched to keep them from slipping forward, and continued downward to encircle the mast below the cheeks.

The lower mast backstays, which were left hanging loose from the clip at the mast cap, should now be fixed at the pin rail in the eyes provided. They should be tied to the eyes, adjusting the tension of the stay to keep the mast true, and the loose end should be tied to the stay at the level of the sheer pole. Similar knots should be made in all the succeeding backstays to give the effect of the bottle screws. Seal the knots with adhesive. Take care not to pull the backstays too tight or the cumulative effect will be to give the mast a very unseamanlike rake. The tendency amongst seamen is rather to have the stays taut, giving a slight forward rake, especially to the top-gallant and royal masts. The ideal is, however, to arrange the tension in each direction so that the masts are straight and at the correct rake.

Backstays

Next come the topmast backstays. There are three on each side, and they are looped over the topmast head as is the case with the shrouds. In the model the odd backstay could be made in one with the odd shroud, thus making three pairs on each side. The cord for the backstays should be cut in 14-in. lengths, for the shrouds in 9-in. lengths, and for the odd shroud and backstay in 11½-in. lengths. The topmast backstays are fixed to the eyes in the pin rail in the manner already described for the lower mast backstays.

The topmast stays, Nos. 44 and 50 in the rigging plan, are now required to complete the rigging of the fore, main and mizzen topmasts. They are similar to those for the lower masts, being double in each case, and they are fitted in the same manner, the only exception being in that for the foremast. The lower end of this is looped around the pegs in the base of the bowsprit and then carried aft to be secured in the vertical portion at the front of the fo'c'sle head. This may be seen in Fig. 71. The two members of the stay are seized together ⅜ in. above the bowsprit, and not left free as was the case with the *Cutty Sark*, and which may be seen in the photograph, Plate 36.

A guide to the size of cord or thread to be used in the rigging will be given when we say that, in the actual ship, the shrouds, stays and backstays up to the topmast are 4⅝ in. circumference, reducing as we go higher, until the royal stays and backstays are only 2½ in. circumference. In the jigger mast the lower shrouds and stays are 3½ in. circumference. Whether the model is rigged with cord, surgical silk, wire, or linen thread, the scale diameter should be adhered to as far as possible. A useful way to measure the diameter is to wind closely a number of coils on a stick, measure the width wound, and divide by the number of coils.

Top-gallant and Royal Masts

The top-gallant and royal masts are made in one piece, as on the actual ship. Three should be prepared to the dimensions given in Fig. 66, the lower end being reduced to $\frac{1}{16}$ in. diameter to fit the hole in the block which represents the trestle-trees. The trucks may be formed of Seccotine or Durofix in the following manner. A pointed instrument is dipped in the adhesive and then held point downwards near the tip of the mast, when the blob of adhesive will transfer itself to the mast and, owing to surface tension, will form itself into a perfect sphere. When almost dry, a slight pressure on the top will flatten it until it forms the flattened sphere typical of the British mast truck. In U.S. ships the mast truck was practically spherical in form.

The topmast caps for holding the top-gallant masts have been described already and should now be fitted in position. The topmast cap backstays should be fitted at the same time, one on each side, being made of one cord 16 in. long and looped over the masthead before fitting the cap. On the fore and main caps an additional cord, 7 in. long, should be inserted under the cap on the after side of the mast to form the main and mizzen royal stays (52). The backstays should be secured to the eyes in the pin rail as with the previous backstays.

Before actually erecting the top-gallant masts, those who wish to do so should drill the masts for the halliards. The holes are just below the point of attachment of the stays. Similar holes should be drilled in the topmasts just below the crosstrees. But I have seen so many models with broken masts, due entirely to drilling these holes, that I prefer not to take the halliard through the mast, but to fix it in a small vertical groove on the fore and after side of the mast, making each portion separate, rather than to weaken the mast by drilling. Of course, in a larger model one need not hesitate to drill the mast ; but even in a ¼-in. scale model of an East India-man which came into my hands recently for repairs, there was a topgallant mast which had broken through this very cause.

Plate 37. Bowsprit from fo'c'sle head
—Archibald Russell

Erection

We can now erect the top-

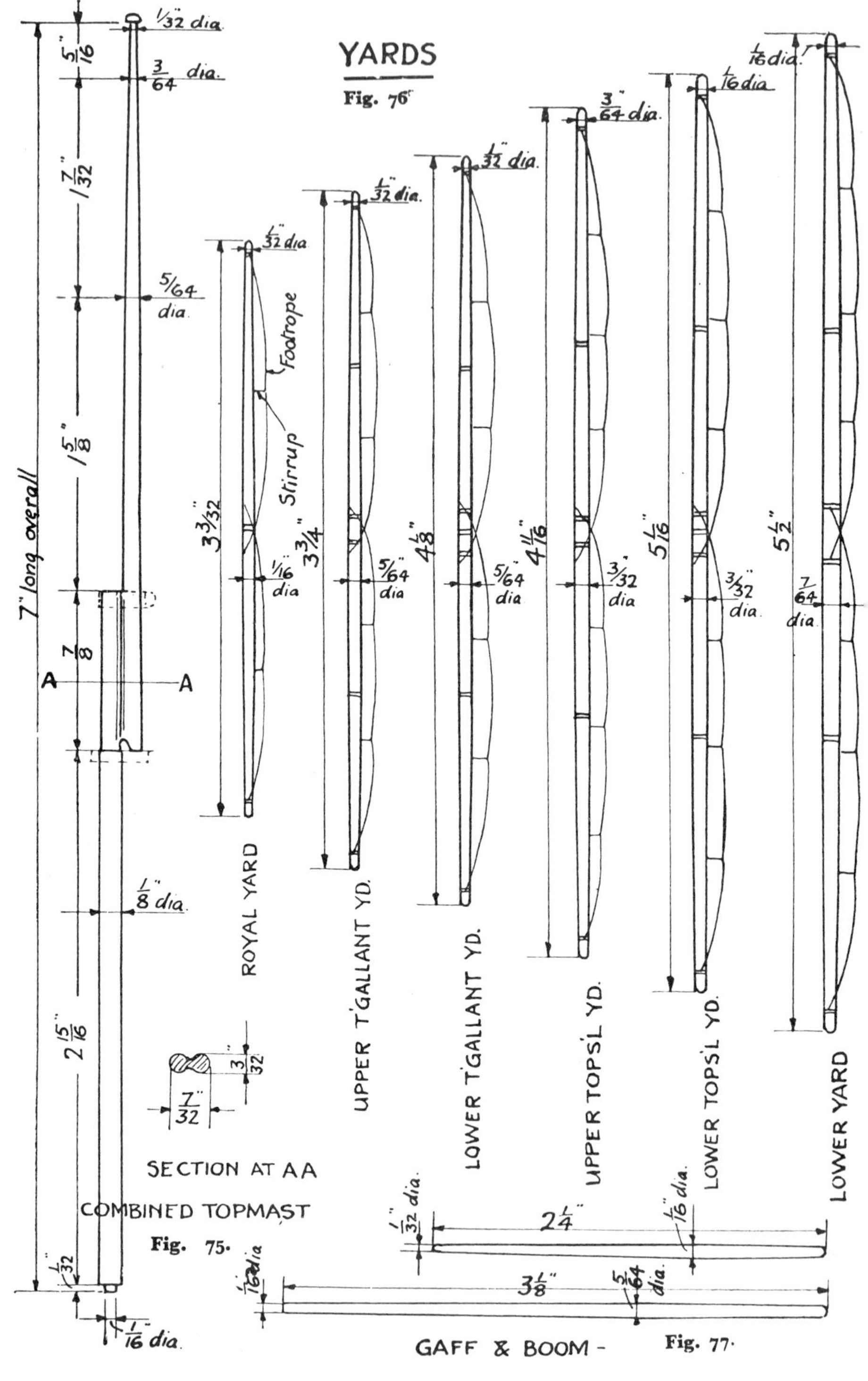
YARDS
Fig. 76.

1/32" dia.
3/64" dia.
5/64 dia.
7" long overall
5/16"
7/32"
1 5/8"
7/8
A   A
1/8" dia.
2 15/16"
1/32"
1/16" dia.

SECTION AT AA
7/32"
3/32"
COMBINED TOPMAST
Fig. 75.

1/32 dia.
5/64 dia.
Footrope
Stirrup
3 3/32"
1/16 dia
ROYAL YARD

1/32 dia.
5/64 dia.
3/4"
UPPER T'GALLANT YD.

1/32 dia.
5/64 dia.
4 1/8"
LOWER T'GALLANT YD.

3/64 dia.
3/32 dia.
4 11/16"
UPPER TOPS'L YD.

1/16 dia
3/32 dia.
5 1/16"
LOWER TOPS'L YD.

1/16 dia.
7/64 dia.
5 1/2"
LOWER YARD

1/32 dia.
1/16 dia
2 1/4"
1/16 dia.

1/16 dia
5/64 dia.
3 1/8"

GAFF & BOOM -   Fig. 77.

SPARS FOR "ARCHIBALD RUSSELL" MODEL — FULL SIZE.   EB.

gallant masts, putting the base of the mast through the clip and inserting the 1/16 in. diameter portion into the hole in the trestle-trees. Next fit the top-gallant shrouds. There are two on each side and they are fixed on the mast at the point where the stays and backstays meet. Bring them down over the ends of the crosstrees, using a spot of Durofix at each point, and secure them to the mast band below. The top-gallant backstays should then be fitted, two on each side, then the main and top-gallant stays (51) which were left hanging loose from the lower mast caps. These should be looped around the mast, resting on the band formed by the attachment of the backstays, and, after getting sufficient tension to hold the mast firm and straight, the end should be seized to the stay on the forward side of the mast.

The foremast stays are somewhat different. The fore-topmast stay (44) is already in position. Immediately over it comes the middle jib stay (45), which is brought down and secured to the bowsprit at the clip for the bobstay. Similarly, the outer jib stay (46) is also looped around the topmast head and brought down to the bowsprit at the point indicated in Fig. 69, 13/16 in. from its outer end. From this point the jib boom guys are led aft, one on each side, to be secured to the bows just under the catheads. Similar guys are led from the end of the jib-boom to the ends of the catheads. These may be seen in the photograph of the bowsprit reproduced on page 97. Plate 37.

The royal backstays should now be fitted on the fore, main, and mizzen masts, one on each side, being made in one length 24 in. long, firmly fixed around the mast at the position indicated in Fig. 66, and led down to the eyes in the pin rail, as were the others. The main and mizzen royal stays (52) which were left hanging from the fore and main topmast caps may now be fitted in the manner and with the correct tension, as already described for the top-gallant stays. In fitting the fore royal stay (48) sufficient length should be allowed to include the jib-boom stay, making the cord about 16 in. long. This should be pegged into the stem close below the bobstay, fixed with a turn around the end of the jib-boom and taken up to the royal masthead, where it is looped around the mast and seized to give the tension necessary to secure the mast at the correct rake. Below the bowsprit the stay should be stretched over the end of the martingale and secured with a spot of Durofix.

Spreaders for Backstays

The spreaders should now be fitted. They are made of split bamboo, 1/32 in. square by 1 in. long, and are provided with slight notches on the outer side opposite the upper backstays. They are glued on top of the

crosstrees at such an angle that they just touch the backstays. If there
is any slackness in the backstays, move the spreaders aft and outward a
little so that when the stays are glued into the notches the tension is
increased somewhat.

The photograph, Plate 38, taken looking up the mast, will be of
interest in this connection. The form of the mast top, the crosstrees, and
the spreaders is well shown, and the backstays can be identified, first the
two from the lower mast cap, then three from the topmast trestle-trees,

Plate 38. " Archibald Russell " looking up main mast

one from the topmast cap, two from the top-gallant mast, and one from
the royal mast, nine in all. The curved end of the after crosstree can be
seen on the port side. The reason for curving the ends of the crosstrees
was to carry the anchorage of the shroud a little farther aft, so that they
help the backstays in counteracting the forward pull of the stays.

Jigger Topmast

The jigger topmast, which is in one piece from the base to the truck,
should be made to the dimensions given in Fig. 66. Normally the weight

of the topmast is taken by a fid through its base which rests on the trestle-trees, but in a model of this size it will be simpler to reduce the base of the mast to $\frac{1}{16}$ in. diameter for a length of about 1/32 in., and to let this fit into a corresponding hole in a tiny piece of three-ply or card about 5/32 in. square, which is glued on top of the trestle-trees. The mast cap is similar to the one already described for the other three topmasts, except that it carries a tiny eye made of wire instead of the yard clip used on the others.

To erect the topmast, first fit the clip in position, at the same time inserting a length of cord between it and the mast on the after side. The ends of this will be used later as the lifts for the gaff. Next put the topmast through the clip and insert the $\frac{1}{16}$ in. diameter portion in the hole provided for it. Now fit the shrouds, two on each side, in the manner already described for the top-gallant shrouds on the other masts. Next in order come the backstays, two on each side. In this connection note that the aftermost backstay is secured to the aftermost or 7th eye on the poop, the top-gallant backstays being secured to the 6th, thus crossing over the topmast backstay. The topmast stay (50) is first fixed around the mizzen lower mast just below the cheeks and then taken to the topmast head where it is looped over the shrouds and backstays, the loop being seized just forward of the mast to give it the correct rake as already described. Next fit the top-gallant backstays, one on each side, and finally the top-gallant stay (51). This will be found hanging from the clip at the mizzen lower mast cap and should be looped over the backstays at the mast-head and secured at the correct tension.

The fitting of the spanker boom and gaff, Fig. 77, is described in the section dealing with the rigging of these spars, see page 116.

Some of the earlier four-mast barques had their lower masts and doublings and the yards painted white. The wooden topmasts and top-gallant masts and the jibboom outside the cap of the bowsprit were scraped and varnished, but the spanker boom and gaff were painted white. There were various fashions, usually depending on the taste or fancy of the master of the ship. In the *Archibald Russell* the masts and yards were painted yellow ochre or a light stone colour, and this was the usual colour for masts and yards in the early years of the 20th century, and is still in general use on the masts of present-day ships. The spike bowsprit which was fitted in the later four-mast barques was usually painted the same colour as the masts and yards.

Whilst on the subject of painting it occurs to me that no mention has been made of the colours of the various deck erections and fittings. Deck houses are usually white, with a strip about 1 ft. wide along the bottom, which may be brown, blue or any dark colour. The same applies to the bulkheads at the break of the poop and fo'c'sle. Bulwarks are usually white on the inside, and wooden companion ways are usually made of varnished teak or mahogany. Cowl ventilators are white with red inside the bell. Anchors and winches are black. Boat skids and boats are white, and often the gunwale strakes of the boats are varnished or dark brown. Hatches are canvas covered when ready for sailing or at sea. Hatch coamings are dark to correspond with the strips on the bulkheads.

Simplified Rigging

When describing the eyes for the backstays—see Figs. 30 and 31 on page 50—we suggested that some builders might prefer to simplify matters by fitting six backstays instead of the nine as on the ship. In this case, one instead of two may be fitted from the lower mast-head, two instead of three from the trestle-trees, and one instead of two from the top-gallant mast-head. This, of course, applies only to the mizzen, main and fore-masts. The jigger mast has only three on each side, and this is not too complicated. The accompanying photograph of my *Cutty Sark* model, Plate 39, shows it at the stage at which we have now arrived with our model of the *Archibald Russell*. It will be seen that the number of backstays was reduced in this model, and, in my opinion, the appearance was not adversely affected, especially when one considers the small scale. The wire clips for the lower topsail yards will be seen. There was none at the topmast caps, as the ship had single top-gallant sails. I might mention that before finishing the model I raised the peak of the spencer gaff, thus improving its appearance very considerably. The vangs for the spanker gaff were not fitted when the photograph was taken.

Topmasts and Top-gallant Masts in One

Before we go further we must describe the method of building the topmasts and top-gallant masts in one. The sketch (Fig. 75) gives the dimensions of the combined mast. The hollow between the masts at the doubling should not be overdone or the wood will split along this line. Clearance should be cut at the bottom of the doubling as shown, to make space for the shrouds. With this method it is impossible to use the wooden knitting-needles recommended for the other method. For my *Cutty Sark* model, in which I made the upper masts in one, I used sycamore, $\frac{1}{8}$ in. thick, selecting a piece with as straight a grain as possible. The block of wood which represents the trestle-trees is drilled $\frac{1}{8}$ in. diameter for the topmast, and is slipped over the lower end and pushed up to the butt of the top-gallant mast. The clip at the cap of the topmast is exactly the same as that described already, as is also the general process of erection.

Yards

The yards should next be made. Fig. 76 gives the dimensions, and as the yards are the same on all three masts, we will require three of each, or eighteen in all. The diameter at the centre diminishes but little for the central half of the yard, most of the tapering being done on the outer quarters of its length.

As to material, if wooden knitting-needles of suitable diameters can be found, well and good, but if not, split bamboo is a very suitable material, especially for the upper yards, as it is very strong and takes on a good finish. Sycamore is also very useful and, after bamboo, I consider it the best material. I have also found cedar very satisfactory, especially that used in pre-war pencils. If the wood is obtained in the form of thin boards, say ⅛ in. thick, it should be split until straight pieces are obtained of the required length. These lengths should then be squared and

Plate 39. Model of " Cutty Sark," $\frac{1}{16}$ in. = 1 foot, with standing rigging only

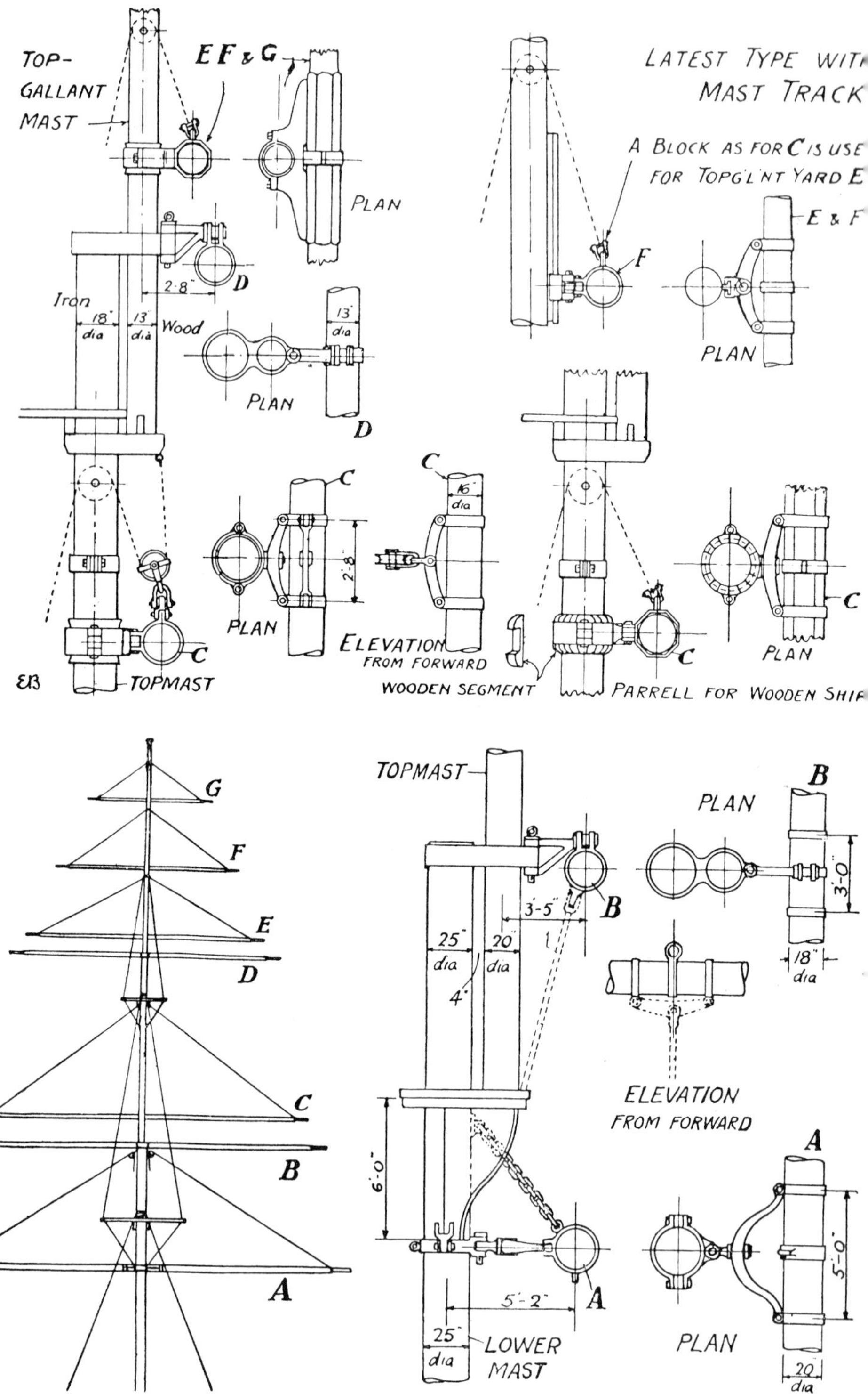

Fig. 78. Typical mast and yard fittings

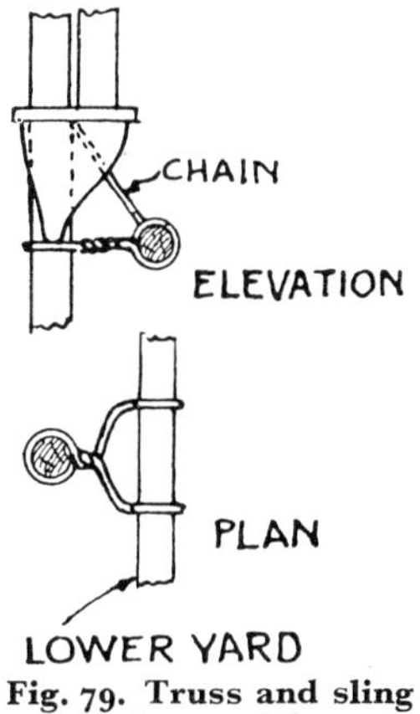

Fig. 79. Truss and sling for model

tapered to the required dimensions before removing the corners. When the corners are removed and the spar is approximately round, one end can be rotated between the finger and thumb while the other is rubbed down with glass-paper. By changing over to the other end and repeating the process, a nicely rounded and tapered spar can be produced. Finish with the finest glass-paper, and finally burnish with the plain side of the paper. The middle portion of the royal yards, which were made of wood, was octagonal in section for two or three feet, but this may well be ignored at our scale.

The line near the end of the yards in Fig. 76 indicates the point of attachment for the braces and lifts, and the portion outside this is technically the yardarm. In older ships the yardarm was much longer than that shown, but when iron and steel yards were introduced, it was shortened very considerably.

The boom and gaff for the spanker should be made to the dimensions given in Fig. 77, the materials and method being the same as for the yards. Note that the greatest diameter for both the gaff and boom is at about one-third of the length from the butt, and that the boom has very little taper as compared with the gaff.

The drawing of the yards shows the foot ropes, but whether or not these are fitted depends on the modeller. They were supported by stirrups, short pieces of wire rope 3 or 4 feet long, which were spliced to the jackstay, a steel bar fixed to the top of the yard for the attachment of the sails.

In the model the stirrups are made of short lengths of fine wire pressed into the yards where shown, and it will be found convenient to make the foot ropes also of wire, soldering them to the ends of the stirrups and fixing the ends to the yards.

The lower, lower topsail, and lower top-gallantsail yards are fixed as to height, being carried from the masts by swivels or cranes. These are shown in detail in Fig. 78 as are also the parrels and halliards for the other yards. In a model of the scale to which we are working, it is almost impossible to show these in detail, although after seeing the amount of detail some builders can introduce into a model, it would be rash to say what is possible and what is not. However, the method we describe will give a reasonable effect and should be well within the capacity of the average modeller.

Erecting the Yards

The sketch (Fig. 79) shows the fitting for the lower yards. It consists of a length of wire 24 gauge by 1⅛ in. long which is fixed around the lower mast at the anchorage for the futtock shrouds. The ends are twisted together and bent to a U-form in plan with the ends of the U pointing forward, and spaced 5⁄16 in. apart. These ends are than bent around the yard. Note that if the model is shown with the sails furled the yards should be squared at right-angles to the centre-line of the hull, whereas if it is to be a water-line model with sails, then the yards should be swung around at about 45 degrees, the upper yards being set at a greater angle to the centre-line of the hull than the lower ones. This is clearly shown in the photograph, Plate 40. This photograph was taken from a 1/32-in. scale model of *Herzogin Cecilie*, made some years ago by the writer, and illustrates clearly the relative setting of the upper and lower yards.

To assist in supporting the great weight of the lower yards, a stout chain was fixed to the mast below the mast top, and shackled to an eye on the top of the yard. This can be represented by a short length of wire, or even a splinter of bamboo, glued in position as shown in Fig. 79.

The lower topsail yard is carried in the loop of wire which was left when fitting the clip at the

Plate 40. Plan view of four-mast barque showing setting of sails

top of the lower masts, the ends of the wire being bent around the central part of the yard. The same fixing is used for the lower top-gallantsail yards, which should be fitted after the upper topsail yards are in position. Additional support is given to the lower topsail yard by a steel strut from the mast top. It is forked and pinned so as to be free to follow the movements of the yard. In the model a piece of wire or split bamboo glued in position will represent it satisfactorily. (See Fig. 80.)

The " Arethusa "

At this stage of our model, the photograph of the *Arethusa*, Plate 41, will be of interest. As many of our readers will remember, she was originally the *Peking*, one of the famous " P " line of sailing ships. A few years before the war she was purchased by the Shaftesbury Homes for Boys to replace their old ship *Arethusa* as a training ship. She was renamed *Arethusa*, and accommodation was built into her between decks, resulting in the row of ports which will be seen in the photograph between her painted ports. During the war her masts were lowered and her yards taken down by the Navy when they took her over for use as a depot ship at Sheerness. However, her spars were taken good care of, and she is now being rigged to her former condition as shown in the photograph. To reduce weight aloft, the upper topsail and top-gallant yards were dispensed with, which accounts for the small number of yards. It will be noticed that her lower and topmasts are in one piece, and that the jigger mast is a single tube from deck to truck. But the fixed yards are in their normal position, the lower topsail yards being carried just where the cap of the lower mast would come in the older style mast. The open wheel on the poop, the flying bridge and gangway between the poop and the bridge deck, and the anchor crane in the fo'c'sle head will be seen in the photograph. Those who are interested, and who are within reach of Upnor, where she is moored, would do well to pay her a visit and study from an actual vessel the various points which we have been discussing.

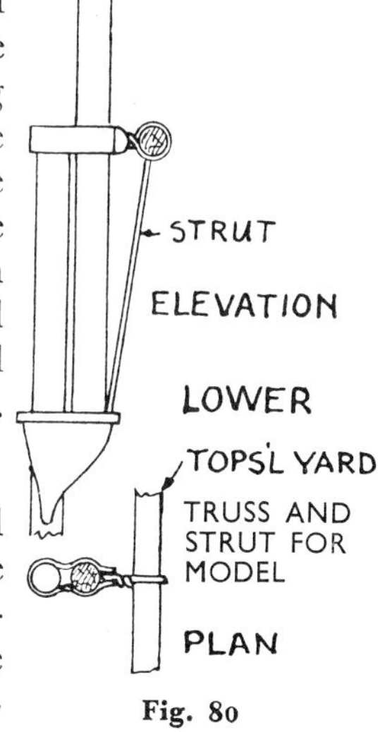

Fig. 80

The Movable Yards

The upper topsail, upper top-gallantsail and royal yards are arranged so that they can be lowered as the sails are furled. They are connected to the mast by means of a parrel. The parrel consists essentially of a ring which en-

Plate 41.   The training ship " Arethusa "

circles the mast and is set at right angles to a clamp ring which encircles
the yard. The ring around the mast is lined with leather which is greased
so that it slides easily on the mast. Its design varies with different ships
and periods. It was shown in detail with other mast and yard fittings in
Fig. 78. As the yards in our model will be shown in either the upper or
lower position and do not need to be movable, the parrels can be represented by a loop of thread tied around the yard at the centre with the
ends tied around the mast in the appropriate position.

Lifts

To assist in describing the rigging for the yards, we have prepared a
scale drawing, Fig. 81, for the model, one half of which shows the yards
with the sails set and the other with the sails removed. The braces and
halliards are not included as they are already shown in the rigging plan,
Fig. 71. The lower yard and the three movable yards are provided with
lifts (68-71). Those for the lower yards (68) are led through blocks at
the mast cap and belayed at the fife rails. This is in order that the yard
may be tilted or " cock-billed " when necessary to clear dock buildings
or other obstructions when the vessel is moored at the quayside. These
blocks may be ignored in our model. The lifts for the three movable
yards should be sufficiently long to support the yard in its position when
lowered. When the yard is hoisted for setting the sails, they are allowed

to hang in a loop on the after side of the yard. The lifts are part of the standing rigging and should be made of black thread.

Halliards

The halliards should next be fitted. These are shown in the rigging plan, Fig. 71, and are numbered 63, 64 and 65. The upper topsail halliard (63) is fixed under the trestletrees, led down to a block at the centre of the yard and up to a sheave in the mast see Fig. 82. As already explained in discussing the masts, I prefer not to weaken the mast by slotting it for a sheave or even to put a hole through it in a model of such a small scale as ours. My method is to glue the halliard into a groove on the fore side of the mast and to continue it on the after side of the mast by gluing a similar but separate thread in the appropriate position. The halliards (64 and 65) for the two upper yards are shackled direct to the yard and led up to the sheave, no double purchase being considered necessary. Up to the end of the last century the halliards were led down the backstays on alternate sides of the ship, but in the *Archibald Russell*, and in most of the later ships, they were led down the mast to a tackle secured to an eye in the deck or to a special winch and then belayed at the fife rails. They may be seen in the view looking up the mast (see Plate 38), the triple block on the right being for the upper topsail yard and the double block on the left for the upper top-gallantsail yard. The tackles at the fife rail are shown in the photograph of the mizzen mast (Plate 43). The triple tackle on the right is for the upper topsail halliard and the double one nearer the mast is for the upper top-gallantsail yard. In a model at our scale I think it will be sufficient to represent them by a single cord for each yard, secured to the fife rail.

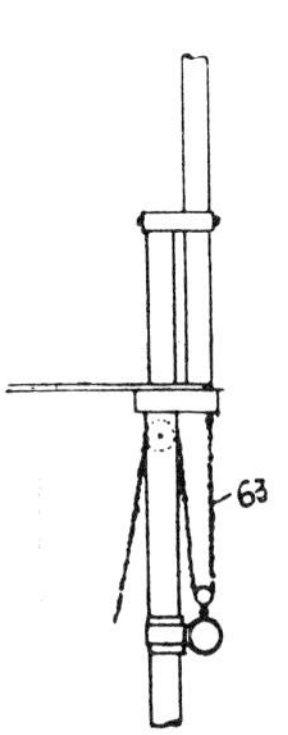

Fig. 81. Upper topsail halliard

Ratlines

Before we proceed further the ratlines should be fitted to the shrouds. In the ship they are spaced about 15 in. apart, but in the model it will be sufficient to space them $\frac{1}{8}$ in. apart, as, unless the ratlines are made of extremely fine thread they will look clumsy if spaced closer. The usual clove hitch fastening at every shroud will also look clumsy. In my *Cutty Sark* model I tied each ratline with a half hitch on the left hand shroud (being right-handed), put a spot of Durofix on each of the other shrouds on a level with the knot, and, stretching the ratline across the

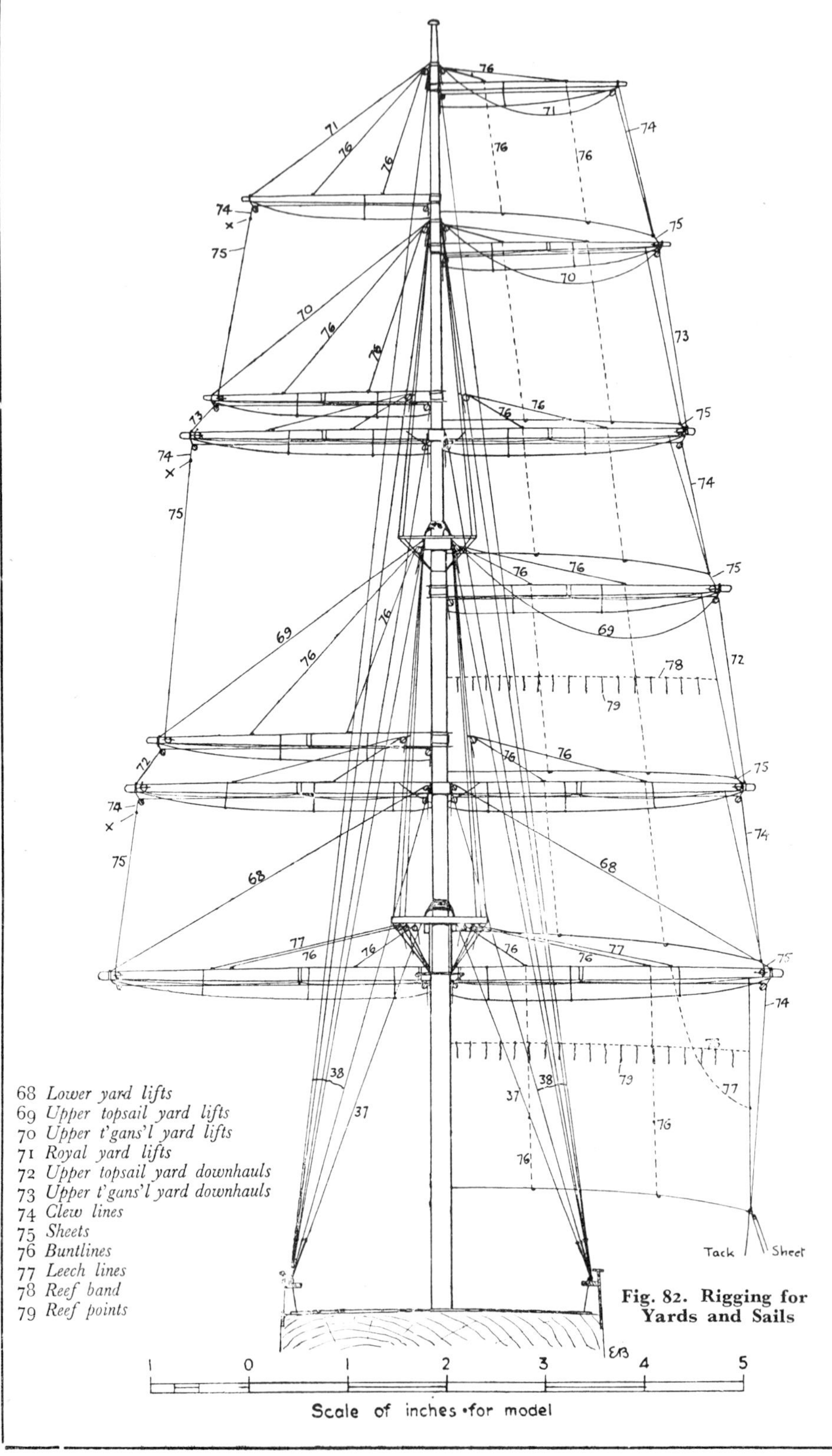

68 *Lower yard lifts*
69 *Upper topsail yard lifts*
70 *Upper t'gans'l yard lifts*
71 *Royal yard lifts*
72 *Upper topsail yard downhauls*
73 *Upper t'gans'l yard downhauls*
74 *Clew lines*
75 *Sheets*
76 *Buntlines*
77 *Leech lines*
78 *Reef band*
79 *Reef points*

Fig. 82. Rigging for Yards and Sails

Plate 42. Brace blocks and shrouds on starboard bulwarks—*Archibald Russell*

shrouds, held it there until the adhesive set. The result was quite satisfactory and gave the correct impression without being clumsy. A few ratlines may be carried aft to the nearest backstays toward the top of the topmast and top-gallant mast shrouds where they would otherwise be too short to be of use.

Poop and Fo'c'sle Head Railings

The railings around the poop and fo'c'sle head have been left until now, as they are apt to be in the way when fixing the rigging. The stanchions are made of fine wire cut into $\frac{1}{4}$-in. lengths. Thirty-one will be required for the poop, and twenty-two for the fo'c'sle head. Their positions are shown in the plan of the deck fittings, Fig. 27. A small hole should be made for each, using a needle or a fine pricker, when they may be pressed in by means of the jig shown in Fig. 46. This automatically regulates the height, which should be $\frac{3}{16}$ in. above the deck. They should be vertical and not necessarily at right angles to the deck line.

The rail around the poop is made of copper wire, 20 s.w.g., which will, of course, be tinned before soldering to the stanchions. After soldering in position the tinning should be scraped off the upper and outer surface, showing the natural colour of the copper. This will tone down in a few weeks until it has the appearance of the mahogany rail. Care must be taken to avoid burning the jigger mast shrouds and backstays when soldering. Essential, a soldering iron (not a blowpipe) and a steady hand.

From the plan, Fig. 27, it will be seen that the railing on the fo'c'sle head passes round inside the lighthouses, and that it is in two portions, being divided just above the bowsprit. This is clearly shown in the photograph, Plate 29. The wide spacing between the stanchions in the photograph and the omission of the lower rail is to facilitate the handling of the anchors. Both the poop and the fo'c'sle railings have two additional rails below the topmost rail. These can be represented by running fine threads around and gluing them in position. As an

Plate 42a. Waterline model of " Archibald Russell " made by E. N. Taylor

additional refinement a fine cord or a strip of Bristol board, 1/32 in. wide, should be glued around the poop, just outside the base of the stanchions, as shown in Fig. 27, already referred to.

Braces

The braces should be fitted in accordance with the rigging plan, Fig. 71. It will be seen that the three lower yards on each mast have pendants. These are fixed to the yards at the yard arm, and those for the lower braces (57) are shorter than those for the topsail braces (58 and 59). The blocks may be represented by blobs of Durofix or Seccotine. When these are almost dry and set they can be squeezed into a shape which gives a fair semblance of a block. The standing end of the tackles for the topsail braces is shackled to a short bumkin on the outside of the hull, as may be faintly discerned in the photograph, Plate 26. The running ends are led through three blocks on the inside of the bulwarks, the ends being led forward and belayed to pins on the pin rail. These blocks are mounted in a frame situated just forward of the main and mizzen shrouds and are clearly shown on the photograph, Plate 42. The arrangement of the mizzen braces is somewhat different. The lower braces have pendants which are shackled to the bumkins, whilst the topsail braces are shackled to eyes on the poop deck. The blocks for the running ends are fixed to the bumkins, and the ends taken through sheaves in the bulwarks at the break of the poop, see Plate 26, and belayed to the pin rail a little further forward. With this arrangement the mizzen braces can be operated from the main deck without having a string of men on the poop. Most builders of our model will find it impossible to reproduce these details in a model of this scale. In my own experience I have found that

Plate 43. Base of mizzen mast looking aft

it is sufficient in a small model to fix the braces to the bumkins and to ignore the fixing of the running ends to the pins on the rail. In a model of ¼ in. scale or over these details should, of course, be included. The upper braces (60, 61 and 62) are single in each case. The running ends are led through blocks at the mast and down to the fife rails, but for a model to our scale it is sufficient to fix the braces to the mast at the appropriate place and to ignore the leads down the mast.

Down-hauls

Under certain conditions, particularly when the ship is experiencing heavy weather, which is the time when yards are likely to be lowered and sails furled, the weight of the yard is insufficient to enable it to over-come the friction and slide down the mast when the halliards are slackened off. To meet this condition down-hauls are provided—see 72 and 73 on Fig. 81. For the upper topsail yard the down-hauls are shackled to the yard arms of the lower topsail yard, led up to the blocks at the yard arms of the upper topsail yard, and along it toward the mast. Near the mast on each side a block is secured to the yard. The down-hauls are led through them and down to the deck, but whether to the fife rails or to the pin rails, I cannot be sure. The action of the down-hauls will be easily understood from the drawing, Fig. 81.

Similar down-hauls are provided for the upper top-gallant yards. For the royal yards the sheets serve as down-hauls, as the yards are lighter and more easily handled than the others.

Clewlines

In a square sail the lower corner on the lee side is known as the clew whilst that on the windward side is the tack. But the ropes controlling these corners are known as clewlines, irrespective of which side of the ship is the windward. The lower edge of the sail is the foot, and the lines controlling it are the buntlines, so called because they used to be more particularly concerned with the centre portion or bunt of the sail. The two outer edges of the sail are known as the leeches, and the lines controlling them are leechlines.

The clewlines (74) are attached to the lower corners of the sails, led up to blocks at the yard arms of the yard which carries the particular sail, along to a pair of blocks at the centre of the yard, and down to the deck to be belayed at the pin rails. Where down-hauls are fitted, as for the upper topsail and upper top-gallantsail yards, the clewlines were dispensed with as, instead of the sail being hoisted up to the yard, the yard was lowered as the sail was furled, the sheet keeping the clew and the tack of the sail secure.

Sheets

The sheets (75) are usually made of chain, from the sail to the point where they are clear of blocks or guide eyes. From the sail they pass through sheaves mounted on the after side of the yard just inside the yard arms, and are led along the yard, passing through an eye at the band halfway between the yard arm and the mast, and to a double block at the centre of the yard and down to the fife rails, usually having a tackle to assist in drawing them tight against the pull of the sail. The sheet block is of a somewhat special design consisting of a pair of steel plates of triangular shape, as shown in Fig. 83.

Buntlines

The function of the buntlines (76) is to draw the foot of the sail up towards the yard and so assist the men who are furling it by relieving them of some of its weight. They are attached to the lower edge of the sail, led up the forward side of the sail through eyes which are built into the sail, through blocks on the yard, up to blocks fitted at suitable positions on the mast or the shrouds (see Fig. 81) and thence down to the pin rails. The clewlines and buntlines are fairly numerous, and in the *Archibald Russell*, as in most of the later ships, the upper lines were grouped together on each side and brought through hoops about 2 ft. diameter fitted to the

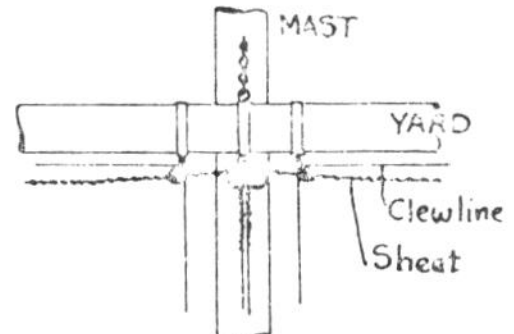

Fig. 83.   Sheet and clewline blocks

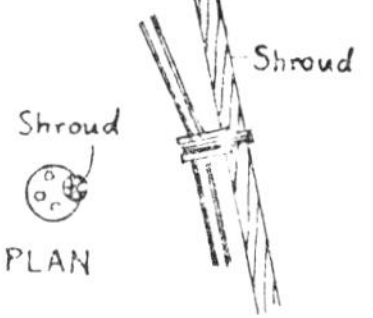

Fig. 84.   Fairleads on shrouds

lower mast cap, one on each side. From there they were led through holes in the mast top, down to fairleads on the shrouds just below the futtock shrouds, down to another set of fairleads just above the rigging screws, and so to the pin rails. The fairleads are, of course, fitted on the inner side of the shrouds, and consist of a block of wood grooved to fit the shroud, to which it is bound by cord, and drilled to take the clewlines or buntlines for which they are provided—see Fig. 84.

Leechlines

The *Archibald Russell* had two leechlines on each of the courses—see (77) on Fig. 82 and photograph on page VIII. These are similar to the buntlines both as to their fittings and leads.

The sheets and tacks for the courses will be described when we are discussing the sails.

We have omitted showing the sails furled along the yards, as in a small model it is neater and better to omit them. When the sails were removed, as for a lengthy stay in port, the clewlines and sheets were shackled together at the points indicated by X on the diagram, Fig. 81, and the lines drawn taut.

Spanker Boom and Gaff

To complete the rigging the spanker boom and gaff should now be fitted. Their length and diameters are given in Fig. 77, and they should be made of the same material and in the same manner as that described for the yards. To secure them to the mast, break the point off a fine needle for a length of 3/32 in. and press the broken end of the fragment into the butt end of the spar, leaving the point projecting for about half its length. The gaff should be fitted first. Referring to the Rigging Plan, Fig. 71, press the point of the needle into the mast at the position shown and attach the topping lifts (54), which were left hanging from the clip at the jigger mast cap, in such a way that the spar is at the correct angle, as shown in the drawing. The upper of the two topping lifts should be continued down to the boom, which may now be fitted, thus becoming the boom topping lift (53). The boom is secured to the mast by the point of the needle in the same manner as that described for the gaff. The spanker sheet (56) is double, the lower blocks being shackled to the poop deck near the rail, one on the port side and one on the starboard. The vangs (55) are also double, and should be secured to the deck near the rails, one on each side.

Flag Halliards

Finally, the ensign halliards (67) and the flag halliards (66) should be fitted. Actually they are double, but unless the very finest silk is used, they should be single cords, as otherwise they are too obtrusive.

Plate 18 is reproduced from a photograph of the *Archibald Russell*, which shows her with painted ports and the sails furled. She is not quite down to her Plimsoll marks, and her sides show signs of having seen some service since she was painted, also her fore royal and mizzen royal yards are down on deck; but she was in her prime when the photograph was taken, and it was this period in her career which we have chosen to represent in our model.

Stand for the Model

If the model has been made with a full hull and is intended to be shown without sails, it is now complete. All that remains to be done is to make a stand to support it, and a case to protect it from dust. The simplest type of stand is that shown in Fig. 11, but if something more elaborate is required, it may be safely left to the discretion of the builder. My personal feeling is that the stand should be simple and secure. The type of stand where the ship is supported on two posts under the keel always makes me feel nervous, although I admit it does exhibit the underwater form without any interruption. However, everyone to his taste.

Case for the Model

The same remarks apply equally to the case. Some people object to putting a model in a case, but I am sure they are wrong. Nothing can prevent dust settling on a model, and sooner or later the model loses its freshness ; then there is the certainty that the rigging, if unprotected, will deteriorate and receive damage. The case should not be too close a fit for the model and the framework should be as light as possible. I heard recently of a case where the glass was ground to a 45-deg. bevel where the edges met and then cemented together without any framing whatsoever. That is the ideal, and the nearer one approaches that the better. Perspex may be used instead of glass but is liable to lose its transparency through being dusted. It has, however, the advantage of being easily fitted and cemented.

Speaking of cases reminds me of a letter I received recently and which contains a warning I would like to pass on. Here is the extract :—

" My 50-ft. to the inch *Archibald Russell* has met with a severe setback due to my own crass stupidity. I finished her last Tuesday, and she looked good. (Having seen some of the correspondent's work, I am sure she would look good.) I proceeded to mount her on a plaster sea, painted the sea, and with a sigh of relief put the glass cover over her. When next I looked at her, some hours later, I nearly wept. The sails were limp, the sheets slack, the masts bowed back, the port boat had fallen away from the davits, the flying bridges were down to deck level between the stanchions, and sea had broken up. In my anxiety to cover her up before any damage occurred, I had not waited for the plaster and paint to dry, and thus the air in the case became super-saturated, and then trouble began."

CHAPTER IX

THE WATERLINE MODEL

SOME modellers of the *Archibald Russell* will undoubtedly prefer to fit it with sails, and show it as a waterline model set in an artificial sea. I have seen models made with the complete hull set on a stand and fitted with sails, but such a model seems all wrong to my mind. Sails suggest speed and action, and to carry them on a model, more especially when it is a small one, the ship should be set in a sea, heeling over to the breeze, and with the sails straining at the sheets.

Then again, there is the question of the material to be used for the sails. To my mind the finest fabric is too coarse for a model of a smaller scale than ¼ in. = 1 ft., and even at that scale fabric must be handled very skilfully if it isn't to look coarse and clumsy. For a model of our scale, viz. : ⅟₁₆ in. = 1 ft., I consider fine bond paper, or the best quality typewriting paper, to be the most suitable material. This can be curled after cutting out the shape of the sails, so as to represent very realistically the effect of the wind. My method is to use a celluloid set-square—anything with a smooth straight edge will do equally well—and, laying the sail on a magazine or other soft pad of paper, press the edge of the set-square across the sail as shown in Fig. 85. The upper edge or the head of the square sails is, of course, kept straight, but from one lower corner to the other the sail should be curved forward and upward, giving a somewhat bag-like effect. When the sails are pressed to shape a thin cord should be glued along the edge to represent the bolt rope. If anything, this should lie on the after side of the sail, but it should be as close as possible to the extreme edge. The bolt rope on the fore and aft sails was always on the port side.

In cutting out the square sails, their dimensions should be taken from Fig. 81, using the scale at the foot of the page. As the sail is secured to the jackstay, which is situated near the top of the yard toward the forward side, the depth of the sail should be measured from this point. A little extra depth should be given to allow for the bellying of the sail. One point to notice in connection with the square sails is that the roach or the curvature at the foot of the lower topsails, the lower top-gallant sails, and the royals is much greater than that on the upper top-sails and top-gallant sails, the reason being that they have to clear the braces and fore-stays. The roach of the three courses is cut to be well clear of the deck-houses and boats.

Fig. 85. Method of curling sails

The reef points, which are found only on the courses and the upper top-sails, may be drawn in pencil, or if preferred, short lengths of thread could be passed through the sails and glued to the sail on each side. If not fixed they will assume all sorts of unnatural positions. Before making the holes for the reef points a narrow strip of thin paper should be glued across the sail on each side to represent the reef bands. The reef points are located at the seams between the cloths of the sails and, therefore, should be spaced approximately ⅛ in. apart in the model.

The buntlines are, of course, a continuation of those from the mast to the yard, already described. They are led through blocks at the top of the yard and carried down the forward side of the sail to be secured at its lower edge. These should be kept in place by rubbing them with adhesive before fixing them along the sail in their correct positions.

Fig. 87 is a diagram showing the sails, with a key which will assist the uninitiated to identify them. The main and mizzen stay-sails (13) were not often used, and may be omitted. Similarly, the main and mizzen royal stay-sails (16) were used only in very light breezes. The photograph, see Plate 44, of a 1/32-in. scale model of *Herzogin Cecilie*, which I made some years ago, shows a typical four-mast barque with sails set. The effect of motion with the sails straining at their sheets will be noticed, as will also the heel of the vessel (don't overdo it!), and the twist on the tiers of square sails. This latter feature is seen also in the photograph of the same model as seen from above (see Plate 40). In this model the sheets of the courses were shown, but not the tacks. These are indicated in the diagram, Fig. 81. The sheets are led aft, the standing end of the tackle being shackled outboard to an eyebolt in the bulwarks just above the line of ports, and the running end taken inboard through a slot in the bulwark and over a sheave fixed to the inside of it. On each side of the ship the sheets should be shown taking the strain of the sail. The tacks are led forward, and on the lee side they will hang slack. On the windward side they share with the sheet the work of keeping the clew of the sail in its forward position, and consequently, should be fairly taut. The pendants for the three lower braces on each mast are considerably longer in the *Archibald Russell* than they were in the *Herzogin Cecilie*. This will be seen on comparing the Rigging Plan, Fig. 71, and the drawing, Fig. 3.

The jib sheets are secured to cleats on the fo'c'sle head, there being a group of four on each side just forward of the light-houses. Those on the lee side will be taut, whereas those on the windward side hang loosely over the stay next below, to be belayed to the cleat without any tension. The same remarks apply to the sheets of the various stay-sails. In the model the sheet on the lee side should be just taut and no more, as excessive tension tends to pull the curvature out of the sail. In this connection I would suggest that when fixing the stay-sails or jibs to their respective stays they should be glued in such a position that they lie practically at right-angles to the centre-line of the ship ; then, when the sheet is attached, the tension pulls the sail back to its normal position, leaving a certain amount of bellying to suggest the effect of the wind. Similarly with the square sails, they should be glued along the upper edge and attached to almost the top of the yard, so that the foot lies well forward of the yard below, see Fig. 86. Then when the sheets are attached the sail has the correct curvature. The sheets should be threaded through the lower corners or clews of the sail, just inside the angle of the bolt rope In connection with the jibs and stay-sails an additional refinement would be to fix a second thread—thinner than the stay and buff-coloured—from the head of the sail to the mast to represent the halliard.

The spanker (8) should be glued to the gaff and to the mast. The foot should be loose, being secured at its after corner, or clew, by means of the outhaul. Three brails, shown in Fig. 87, should be represented by threads glued on each side. Actually they are reeved through blocks on each side of the mast and led down to a spider band at the foot.

The jigger top-sail (9) is hooped to the mast between the top-mast stay and the lower-mast cap. The head is controlled by the halliard, which is led through a block and down the mast. The aftermost angle or the clew, and the tack, are secured by their respective tackles, that for the clew being led through a sheave in the gaff, along the gaff and down the mast, while that for the tack, which is on the port side of the spanker, is led to a block on the mast and down to the spider band.

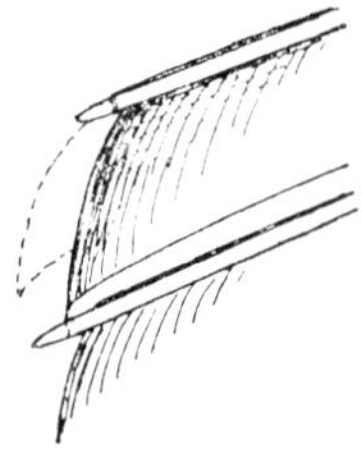

The Base or Sea

The base of a water-line model gives considerable scope for the artistic taste and ability of the modeller. If the model is shown in full sail the waves should

Fig. 86

not be too pronounced, just long, easy rollers. Under such conditions it is unlikely that the waves would have white crests, but for the sake of effect a few white crests could be shown. Referring to the plan view, Plate 40, in which the wind is assumed to be on the starboard quarter, the line of the rollers is approximately the same as that of the lower yards. A reasonable bow wave should be shown, but here again, don't overdo it. The wake will, of course, be white and frothy, with the waves spreading on either side. On the windward side some broken water may be shown with a wave or two breaking up the side of the ship. Whenever the water-line ship modeller has the opportunity of a sea trip, even if it is only the crossing to the Continent, he will have endless opportunities of studying the wave formation about the ship if he takes the trouble to walk around the ship and watch the various effects fore and aft, and to note the difference between the waves on either side.

The base should be made of a piece of wood approximately 24 in. long by 8 in. wide by $\frac{5}{8}$ in, thick. Yellow pine, if obtainable, is probably the best wood to use, but, failing that, any soft cheesy wood with a close grain is suitable ; a hard wood is not necessary. After squaring the wood, cut a recess in the centre to receive the hull, which, as already explained,

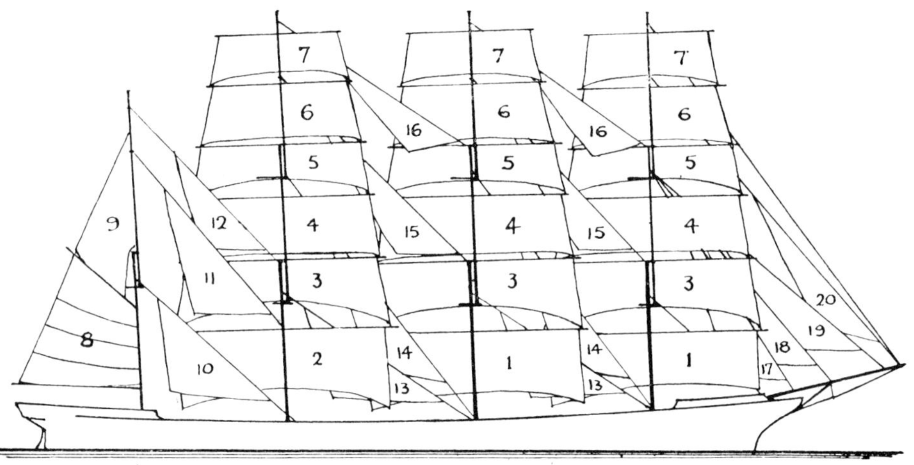

Fig. 87. Diagram of sails

(1) Fore and Main Course.
(2) Mizzen Course or Cro'jack.
(3) Fore, Main and Mizzen Lower Topsail.
(4) ,, ,, ,, ,, Upper ,,
(5) ,, ,, ,, ,, Lower T'gan's'l.
(6) ,, ,, ,, ,, Upper ,,
(7) ,, ,, ,, ,, Royal.
(8) Spanker.
(9) Jigger Topsail.
(10) ,, Staysail.

(11) Jigger Topmast Staysail.
(12) ,, T'gallant ,,
(13) Main and Mizzen Staysail.
(14) ,, ,, ,, Topmast Staysail.
(15) ,, ,, ,, T'gallant ,,
(16) ,, , ,, Royal ,,
(17) Fore Topmast Staysail.
(18) Inner Jib.
(19) Outer Jib.
(20) Flying Jib.

has been cut off flat about ¼ in. below the water-line. The bottom of the recess should be inclined athwarthship, as shown in the section, Fig. 88, to give the required heel to the ship. For carving the sea use a gouge, not too flat, and work from crest to crest, rather than along the troughs. The small hollows so formed suggest the irregular surface of the water very effectively.

Next, place the ship in the recess, securing it in position by means of a screw fore and aft, screwing them in from below. Then with plastic wood fill in any space which may be left between the recess and the sides of the hull, and form the bow wave and the waves along the sides, working the plastic wood between finger and thumb. When set it can be carved to blend with the normal wave formation. Plastic wood sets with a certain roughness, and advantage should be taken of this to suggest the broken water alongside the ship and on the crests of the waves. A little should be worked on to the top of the ridges where it is desired to show broken water.

In painting the sea one usually wishes to suggest a blue sky and sunny conditions. This results in a sea with deep-blue in the troughs, shading towards green at the top of the rollers, and culminating in white for the broken water of the crests and along the sides of the vessel. On the other hand, one may prefer to show the model under stormy conditions. In this case much less sail should be set, in the extreme case cutting down to the six top-sails. One of the most effective water-line models I have seen is that of the *Herzogin Cecilie* in the Deutsches Museum, Munich, showing her under just these conditions, with the figures of over sixty officers, cadets and men on the deck and on the yards shortening sail. The model was about six feet long and was a magnificent piece of work. The sea was grey and threatening, as was appropriate. Across the passage there was a similar model of the five-masted ship *Preussen* with all sail set and on a pleasant sea of blue and green. Both models were very impressive in their different ways. The modeller is strongly advised to experiment, both with the carving and the painting, on a piece of scrap wood before commencing work on the wood which is to represent the sea.

Many water-line modellers, especially sailors, prefer to make their seas in putty, but my objection to it is the smooth, oily effect which seems to result. A wooden sea such as here described has a freshness and naturalness which I have never seen produced by any other means.

That, I think, completes the instructions for making the model of the *Archibald Russell*, both with and without sails. I have tried to describe fully all the points which are likely to arise in modelling both the *Archibald*

Russell and other four-mast barques but if there is anything not quite clear to any of my readers, a letter to the author, c/o *Ships and Ship Models*, will always have attention.

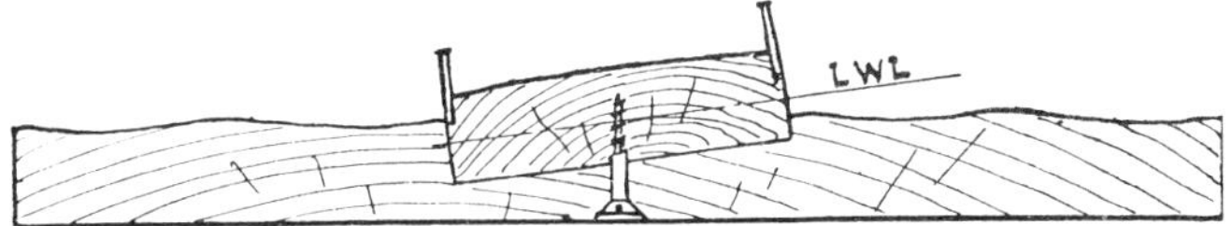

Fig. 88. Section through hull as set in base board

Plate 44. A waterline model of the "Herzogin Cecilie." Scale 1/32 in. = 1 foot

LIST OF FIGURES

TABLE OF DIMENSIONS
Four-masted barques mentioned in this book

Built	Name	Tons	Length ft.	Breadth ft.	Depth ft.	Builders
1905	Archibald Russell	2354	291.3	42.9	24.0	Scott, Greenock.
—	Arethusa (*see Peking*)	—	—	—	—	—
—	Beatrice (*see Routenburn*)	—	—	—	—	—
—	Bellands (*see Forteviot*)	—	—	—	—	—
1901	Brilliant	3765	—	—	—	Russell, Port Glasgow
1889	Carradale	2085	285.7	41.0	23.7	Stephen, Glasgow.
1902	Daylight	3698	351.5	49.1	28.2	Russell, Port Glasgow
1890	Fascadale	2803	285.7	41.0	23.7	Stephen, Glasgow.
1891	Forteviot	3145	317.3	46.0	25.2	Potter, Liverpool.
1853	Great Republic	4555	335.0	53.0	38.0	Donald McKay, Boston, U.S.A.
1902	Herzogin Cecilie	3242	324.1	46.0	23.8	Rickmers Akt. Ges., Bremerhaven.
1894	Herzogin Sophie Charlotte	2591	276.3	43.1	25.4	do. do.
1897	Hougomont	2428	292.4	43.2	24.0	Scott, Greenock.
1895	Inverness-shire	2307	282.9	42.8	24.7	Duncan, Glasgow.
1892	John Ena	2842	312.9	48.1	25.0	do. do.
1892	Jordanhill	2291	278.4	42.0	24.2	Russell, Port Glasgow
1908	L'Avenir	2738	278.2	44.8	26.5	Rickmers.
1892	Lawhill	2942	317.4	45.0	25.1	Thompson, Dundee.
1892	Lyderhorn	2914	311.2	42.4	25.5	Oswald M. Haven.
1894	Lynton	2531	299.8	43.7	24.5	Evans, Liverpool.
1891	Muskoka	2357	300.5	42.0	24.7	Richardson, Duck, Stockton-on-Tees.
1892	Olivebank	2824	326.0	43.1	24.5	Mackie & Thomson, Glasgow.
1891	Owenee	2432	309.0	42.0	24.6	Richardson, Duck, Stockton-on-Tees.
1905	Pamir	3020	316.0	46.0	26.2	Blohm & Voss, Hamburg.
1891	Pass of Melfort	2346	298.8	44.0	24.5	Fairfield, Glasgow.
1884	Pegasus	2631	314.0	42.3	24.9	Potter, Liverpool.
1911	Peking	3191	315.0	47.0	28.0	Blohm & Voss.
1882	Port Jackson	2132	286.2	41.1	25.2	Hall, Aberdeen.
1920	Priwall	3185	323.1	47.1	26.3	Blohm & Voss.
1893	Queen Margaret	2144	275.0	42.2	24.0	McMillan, Dumbarton.
1889	Rapahannock	3054	—	—	—	A. Sewall, Bath, Maine, U.S.A.
1884	Reliance	2631	313.7	42.3	24.9	Potter, Liverpool.
1892	Roanoke	3347	311.2	49.2	29.2	A. Sewall.
1881	Ross-shire	2257	289.1	41.2	24.4	Scott, Greenock.
1881	Routenburn	1997	289.7	42.2	23.9	Steele, Glasgow.
1890	Shenandoah	3154	299.7	49.1	29.9	A. Sewall.
1887	Sindia	3068	329.3	45.2	26.7	Harland & Wolff Ltd., Belfast.
1892	Springburn	2655	296.0	45.6	25.7	Barclay, Curle & Co., Glasgow.
1891	Susquehanna	2591	273.6	45.1	28.0	A. Sewall.
1877	Tweedsdale	1403	244.4	37.4	22.6	Barclay, Curle & Co., Glasgow.
1907	Viking	2952	293.8	45.9	23.8	Burmeister & Wain, Copenhagen.
1882	Walter H. Wilson	2461	308.1	42.7	24.9	Harland & Wolff Ltd., Belfast.
1891	Wanderer	2903	309.0	46.0	25.8	Potter, Liverpool.